The Long Diaconate: 1987-1994

women deacons and the delayed journey to priesthood

Leslie J. Francis

and

Mandy Robbins

First published in 1999

Gracewing
2 Southern Avenue
Leominster
Herefordshire HR6 0QF

All rights reserved. No part of this publication may be reproduced, stored in a retrieval system, or transmitted in any form, or by any means, electronic, mechanical, photocopying, recording, or otherwise, without the written permission of the publisher.

© Leslie J. Francis and Mandy Robbins
1999

The publication of this book has been supported by a grant awarded by the Book Publishing Committee of Trinity College Carmarthen.

The right of the editors and contributors to be identified as the authors of this work has been asserted in accordance with the Copyright, Designs and Patents Act 1988.

UK ISBN 0 85244 472 9

Typesetting by Anne Rees

Printed by Anthony Rowe Ltd
Chippenham, Wiltshire, SN14 6LH

Contents

Preface	v
Introduction	1
1 Call to ministry	51
2 Selection	62
3 First appointment	70
4 Training incumbent	79
5 Last appointment as deacon	88
6 Last incumbent as deacon	98
7 Clerical colleagues	107
8 Parishioners	115
9 Family	122
10 Friends	129
11 Collaborative ministry	137
12 Stress in ministry	144
13 Satisfaction in ministry	152
14 Public role	160
15 Pastoral role	166
16 Social role	174
17 Liturgical role	181
18 Inclusive language	188
19 Church's attitude to women	196
20 Ordination debate	204
21 Legislation and ecumenism	212
22 Bishops and beyond	221
Conclusion	229
Endnotes	239
Index	248

Preface

The Long Diaconate is concerned with the experiences of those women who were ordained to the diaconate within the Church of England between 1987 and 1992, when the Church of England was still debating whether or not to ordain women to the priesthood. Over 1200 women deacons took part in our study. We wish to record to those individuals our deep appreciation for their cooperation and for the trust they showed in us. We hope that they will now recognise their own voices coming through the story which we are telling on their behalf.

The study itself owes its origin and completion to the work of the Centre for Empirical Theology established at Trinity College Carmarthen. Empirical theology is concerned with examining the context and consequences of the church's life and mission with the clear objectivity of the social sciences. This study concerning women deacons is part of a family of studies concerning clergy from Anglican, Roman Catholic, Methodist and Pentecostal Churches underway at the centre. Other studies are concerned with children and young people across the denominations, church growth, and church leaving. We are grateful to the Principal of Trinity College and to the College Governors for making research of this nature available to the churches. We are also grateful to those who sponsor our projects. Analysis of qualitative data from *The Long Diaconate* project was sponsored by the British Academy.

Finally we wish to record our gratitude to Diane Drayson for help in shaping the text.

Leslie J. Francis
Mandy Robbins
Trinity College Carmarthen
August 1999

Introduction

In 1987 the Church of England admitted women to the diaconate for the first time.[1] These ordinations signalled a significant change in the Church of England's attitude toward the ministry of women. They also signalled a significant change in the Church of England's attitude toward the diaconate.[2]

For generations the diaconate in the Church of England had been treated as a transitionary period between laity and priesthood. Men made deacon one year could generally expect to be ordained priest the next year, unless something very seriously went amiss with their spirituality or with their morality. In other words, the Church of England had lost the sense of the permanent diaconate as a ministry in its own right.[3]

In 1987 when the first women were made deacon in the Church of England they were made deacon in a church which had neither provision to ordain women to the priesthood nor a secure theology of a permanent diaconate. In the absence of such theological underpinning, these women were left, in conjunction with those with whom they shared ministry, to work out in practice their role as permanent deacons. Many of these women entered the order of deacons in the firm hope that their diaconate, too, was to be seen as a transitory period between laity and priesthood. Yet they knew full well that in 1988, when men who had been admitted to the diaconate in 1987 were priested, they would not be called forward to stand alongside those men for the laying on of hands. They had entered on that *long diaconate* which terminated only after considerable struggle and pain in 1994 when the Church of England ordained women to the priesthood for the first time.[4]

According to the official figures published by the Church of England in the series *Church Statistics*[5] the following numbers of women were ordained as deacon to the stipendiary ministry between 1987 and 1993: 64 in 1987, 67 in 1988, 56 in 1989,

79 in 1990, 72 in 1991, 67 in 1992 and 56 in 1993. At the same time the numbers of women ordained as deacon to non-stipendiary ministry were as follows: 39 in 1987, 45 in 1988, 44 in 1989, 42 in 1990, 49 in 1991, 74 in 1992 and 51 in 1993.

The Long Diaconate is about the experiences of these women deacons immediately prior to the ordination of the first women to the priesthood in the Church of England. Their story is based on the replies of 1,139 women deacons, licensed within the Church of England, to a detailed questionnaire sent out during January 1994.

There are three good reasons for listening to the experiences of these women deacons five years after their stories had been recorded. First, it may have been too painful and too distracting to tell the tale in 1994 amid the rejoicing and the trauma of the first ordination to the priesthood. The need then was to get on and build the vision, not mull over the carefully compiled data. Second, however, it is now important that the church does not forget the recent past and ignore the implications and consequences of the long diaconate. It is against this background that the current place of women priests needs to be assessed, for significant inequalities still remain. Third, when the present study was set up in 1993 we had a keen eye on the future. The research was designed in such a way that it could be replicated in a decade's time. If the church should be in any sense interested in the impact which ordination to the priesthood has made on the ministry of women, it needs a securely founded benchmark against which to assess that impact. This study was designed to provide just such a benchmark. So we now need to test whether the church is interested in using that benchmark.

Previous research

When we set up the project in 1993 our first aim was to develop a clear map of the issues with which we should be concerned. Our first step was to take a careful look at the international research literature on women in ministry.

We discovered that quite a large number of empirical studies, employing both quantitative and qualitative research methods, had been conducted among clergywomen and their congregations within the USA. In comparison a much smaller number of studies had been undertaken in the UK and Canada. These studies, within the different cultures, have concentrated on four main areas: clergywomen and their ministry, including biographical accounts; the congregation and the clergywomen; comparing and contrasting the experiences of clergywomen and clergymen; the employment of psychometric tests on clergywomen and clergymen. Accordingly, the following review provides a brief synopsis of the international research literature by country which is sub-divided according to the four main areas identified above. Within each of these sub-sections the research is ordered chronologically by publication date.

USA: clergywomen and their ministry

Cardwell[6] examined reasons for clergywomen's failure or success in ministry. The method of sample selection for this study was subjective, based on one person's knowledge of a seminary group of students who were in active ministry from the year of 1958. This sample of clergywomen was divided into two groups, those who were successful in ministry and those who were unsuccessful. No criteria on which the selection was made are given. A questionnaire which contained the Theological School Inventory,[7] the Minnesota Multiphasic Personality Inventory,[8] the Adjective Check List[9] and the California Test of Mental Maturity[10] was employed. Cardwell concludes that those clergywomen who are most successful in ministry tend to be of higher intelligence, have a better self image, are open to feelings, and have leadership ability.

Carroll, Hargrove and Lummis[11] employed four methods of data collection. First, they conducted telephone interviews with 636 clergywomen, representing a response rate of 70%. Second, they conducted postal questionnaires among 679 clergywomen, representing a response rate of 59%. Third, they conducted telephone interviews with 120 clergymen, representing a response rate of 60%. Fourth, 350 of the clergywomen and 125 of the clergymen distributed questionnaires to three of their main lay people within their own parish, representing a 53% response rate. The findings demonstrate that clergywomen are more likely to be found in assistant roles and smaller parishes. Clergywomen are also likely to be paid less. In general both clergymen and clergywomen tend to get on well with parishioners and for both a relaxed ministry style is preferred. The laity tend to see clergywomen as equal to or better than clergymen in all areas of ministry apart from that of managing the churches' finances. This professed acceptance of clergywomen was not found to be necessarily reflected in the willingness of the laity to call a clergywoman to minister in their own congregation.

Coger[12] conducted twelve in-depth interviews of United Methodist Church clergywomen who attended one conference and who all worked with the same bishop. The bishop decides where clergy will take up their appointment and can send them anywhere within his jurisdiction. Coger's aim was to explore clergywomen's support networks and levels of stress. Coger found that the importance of support networks is to some extent dependent on geographical location and further that they have to be worked at in order to be successfully maintained. Coger found that stress levels are related to comparability between the congregation and clergywomen. There can also be the added stress of being a token woman.

Carpenter[13] was concerned specifically with the situation of black clergywomen, in view of the fact that a proportionally higher number of black women were entering seminary than white women. A questionnaire was sent to a sample of black clergywomen who had graduated from seminary with a Master of Divinity and a 45% response rate was achieved (n=120).

Carpenter found that over half of the women had transferred denomination, with a significant number moving from traditionally black churches to predominantly white churches. In total 61% were now working in predominantly white mainline Protestant denominations. Nearly one third of this group had transferred because of the perception of greater opportunities. Carpenter notes that black clergywomen are moving as they feel discriminated against in the traditionally black churches.

Long Ice[14] conducted seventeen in-depth, semi-structured interviews with clergywomen. Long Ice examined four main issues: self-image, notions of ministry, view of institutional settings, and ultimate perceptions. In conclusion she stated that clergywomen rely on a personal approach to ministry based on 'egalitarian negotiation skills', using the 'primary criterion of responsible caring'.

Nesbitt[15] examined 1,158 male and female clergy career paths. The clergy were from the Unitarian Universalist Association and the Episcopal Church. Nesbitt categorised the jobs held by clergy into nine hierarchical levels. She combined this categorisation with a number of background factors such as age at ordination and level of education, as well as gender. Against this background, Nesbitt found that there is operating what she terms a *dual ordination tract*. Nesbitt suggests that these two tracts in the ordained ministry in effect serve to minimise the effect of ordained women on the overall ministry of the church. The main result of this is that women are to a large extent kept out of those jobs which are deemed to carry a high profile or prestige.

The research services section of the Presbyterian church[16] surveyed all the ordained women on the address list of the Women's Ministry Unit. They achieved a 68% response rate (n=1,468). Although the findings in themselves are interesting, there is no clear attempt made to analyse these findings within this report. Over a quarter of the women are solo pastors, with 23% being in associate pastor positions and nearly one third part-time. Their gender is seen as having a positive effect among their congregation but a mixed effect among fellow clergy. Nearly 90% of the clergywomen felt satisfied in their ministry position, although 46% had thought about leaving ministry and a further four out of five had experienced sexism. Half of the clergywomen had changed their goals since entering ministry for a number of reasons, including changes in understanding of gifts and lack of geographic mobility due to family commitments.

USA: the congregation and the clergywomen

The Contact Hypothesis[17] proposes that contact with a person who is the subject of prejudice will result in the person holding that prejudice comparing what they believe to be true with the reality they find and adjusting their prejudice accordingly. At the beginning of the 1980s Lehman examined the contact hypothesis in relation to the rising numbers of clergywomen in the United States.[18] He examined the corresponding levels of congregational acceptance in relation to contact with a woman priest/minister. It seemed logical to project that members of a congregation who come into favourable contact with a clergywoman would, as a result, be more willing to accept another woman in such a position within their church. This has been applied to clergywomen in the United States. However, there has been no support for the contact hypothesis in any of these studies. Rather they have shown that if individual members of a congregation change their view in favour of clergywomen as a result of contact it does not necessarily mean they are more accepting of clergywomen as a group.

Organisational maintenance theory can be defined as the method(s) employed by members of an organisation in order that the organisation might maintain its viability. Church members have a vested interest in contributing in this way in order that their congregation and to a lesser extent their denomination remain in existence. Lehman[19] found that the appointment of a woman could have a perceived positive effect on organisational maintenance in a certain situation, that is in a declining church. However, in the main laity are all too ready to accept that the proposal of a woman pastor will meet with resistance with the majority of the members of their congregation. Because churches feel vulnerable the members will try to avoid confrontation even with a small group within their own structure and this works against churches considering calling a clergywoman.

Royle[20] conducted a comparison between clergywomen and clergymen who held similar job positions, had a similar level of experience and length of time in their present appointment to see if her perception of positive attitudes to women clergy was being extended to supportive behaviour from congregations. From four mainline Protestant denominations 129 pairs of clergy were selected, making a total sample of 258. Membership and financial indicators would suggest that women are being accepted and supported. However, Royle does acknowledge that this study, by its nature, is only able to examine those women who have been successfully placed.

USA: clergywomen and clergymen

Bock[21] used census data from the USA to compare demographic information of clergywomen and clergymen. Bock hypothesised that clergywomen will find themselves marginalised by the clerical profession. Bock found that from 1960 the clergywomen tended to be older than the clergymen. He also found that women who obtain high educational standards are more likely to enter a professional job other than ministry, and that clergywomen are less likely to be married than clergymen.

Malony[22] reports on three studies which examined clergy stress. The second of these three studies examined seminarians, priests, Protestant clergy, rabbis and men religious. Of the total sample of 596, 48.3% were female. The data demonstrated that the women tended to report a higher level of stress. However, given that the sample consists of rather a mixed group of religious affiliations it is possible that, if affiliation were controlled for, there would be no significant differences between the men and women in this sample. Unfortunately this information is not available within this overview of the study.

Lehman[23] conducted structured telephone interviews with ministers working in congregations of four mainline Protestant denominations. The sample consisted of 100 clerics from each of the four mainline denominations, made up of 50 male and 50 female participants. Lehman planned to supplement these telephone interviews by two further studies: one involving a hundred ministers from racial or ethnic groups, and the other involving ten senior female ministers from each of the four denominational groups. In the event, Lehman was unsuccessful in obtaining ten senior female ministers for one of the denominations. Each person interviewed was asked to name two key members of their laity who were then interviewed to see how far the ministers' perceptions of their own ministry were matched by that of their congregation. Lehman concluded that on balance clergymen and clergywomen are more alike than different. While there are gender differences in ministry styles, these differences are small and only present under certain conditions. Furthermore, on balance the laity agreed with self assessments made by the clergymen and clergywomen.

USA: psychometric tests

Flagg[24] used the short form of the Texas Social Behaviour Inventory[25] and the Bem Sex Role Inventory[26] among 114 Protestant clergywomen. The results demonstrated that the scores were not significantly different from the control group of Stanford students with regard to the Bem Sex Role Inventory. However, Flagg found that those clergywomen who were classified as androgynous or masculine on the Bem Sex Role Inventory scored higher on the self-esteem measure than those who were classified as feminine or undifferentiated.

Ekhardt and Goldsmith[27] used the Personality Research Form[28] and the Bem Sex Role Inventory among 204 male and female seminarians and 98 graduate education students. The results demonstrated that there were greater similarities between male and female seminarians then between male and female graduate education students.

UK: clergywomen and their ministry

As part of the production of the report *Deacons Now*,[29] all women serving as deacons in four dioceses in the Midlands received a questionnaire. A response rate of 86% was achieved. Of this sample 76% had been deaconesses before entering the diaconate. The women deacons frequently reported that being an ordained deacon had meant a greater recognition of their ministry, which they felt had a positive effect on their work. In response to the question of raising complaints with their fellow clergy, 55% said they had done so. Such complaints tended to be dealt with by discussion with colleagues or an immediate superior as appropriate.

Penfold's[30] edited volume contains nine personal accounts of women's ministry. These women come from both the Church of England and the Free Churches and can be classed as evangelical in their church tradition. Penfold points out that this group of women have tended not to pursue the traditional route to ordained ministry, even where it was available to them.

Treasure's[31] study is based on thirty eight interviews of women deacons. Each interviewee was assured of anonymity with names and places changed when accounts of the interviews were documented. Treasure has edited the interviews into five subject headings: women at work, being changed, priesthood and 'promotion', making changes, and staying power. Each chapter contains verbatim transcripts of sections of interviews with women deacons together with Treasure's interpretation. Treasure concludes that admitting women to what was, in effect, a permanent diaconate has clouded the distinctiveness of the order of deacons as the women were often perceived as priests in waiting. From the interviews she concluded that the women do not feel that priesthood will make a great deal of difference to the implementation of their ministry, except sacramentally.

UK: the congregation and clergywomen

The local/cosmopolitan dichotomy was first applied to mainstream Christianity in the USA by Roof.[32] Roof ascertained that there was a link between conservative religiosity and prejudice. Lehman took Roof's theory and methodology and applied it with particular reference to congregational receptivity to clergywomen. Lehman's hypothesis followed Roof in that he believed congregational members who are local in orientation will exhibit a greater tendency to discriminate against clergywomen than those who are more cosmopolitan in outlook. This hypothesis was applied to a major study of English church members carried out by Lehman between 1983 and 1984.[33] The findings supported the hypothesis, that those members of congregations who hold a local orientation are more willing to discriminate against clergywomen.

Nason-Clark[34] employed both qualitative and quantitative research methods among three mainline Protestant denominations in Southern England. A random sample of clergy was selected and an 88% response rate was achieved (N=550). Of the 550 respondents, all completed questionnaires and 338 completed interviews. Where appropriate, the spouse was interviewed as well. The response rate for the sub-group of spouses was 96%. Deaconesses were interviewed on their own. The response rate for women ministers as a subgroup was 93%. Nason-Clark examined the clerical attitudes toward appropriate roles for women in church and society. Broadly speaking two groups emerged. Group one had a conservative sex role position, conservative views of the bible and were more likely to be Baptists, Anglicans, clergymen, Catholic or Evangelical rather than middle of the road in their theology. Those falling into this first group tended to have left school with no qualifications and tended not to be in favour of women priests. Group two is largely the opposite of the first group. Furthermore, those falling into group two are more likely to be clergymen with an employed wife or clergy wives with experience of paid employment.

Lehman[35] applied the contact hypothesis in England. These studies provided similar results to those obtained in the USA. Lehman found that contact with a clergywoman leads to the congregation being more favourable to the clergywoman involved with their congregation but does not tend to change the overall attitude to a favourable perception of clergywomen as a group.

UK: clergywomen and clergymen

Nason-Clark[36] interviewed 550 male and female clergy in England. She found that clergywomen differed from clergymen in three main areas. The first area concerned their personal characteristics: for example, clergywomen are more likely to be single and if they marry do so later in life. The second area concerned their reasons for choosing the clerical profession: for example, personal experience was a stronger factor in their decision. The third area concerned the factors they find both rewarding and costly in their ministry: for example, the clergywomen found the time constraints costly. Nason-Clark sums up the differences between the clergywomen and clergymen in the following way, 'In essence, women in ministry appear to be more other-centred than their male colleagues.'

Aldridge[37] employed both qualitative and quantitative research methods. A postal questionnaire was sent to all Anglican parochial clergy in one diocese, from which an 82.4% response rate was received. This was followed up with interviews with forty clergymen, and with eighteen deaconesses and accredited laywomen. Aldridge found that over half of the clergymen surveyed (53.9%) were in favour of women priests. However, Aldridge states that it is possible for a clergyman to insulate himself from the ordained ministry of women and, because of this, the issue is not necessarily a major concern to their working lives.

UK: psychometric tests

Francis[38] used the Eysenck Personality Questionnaire[39] among 155 male and 97 female Anglican ordinands. The female ordinands' scores on the extraversion, neuroticism and psychoticism scales are closer to the male population norms than to the female population norms. The male ordinands' scores on the extraversion scale are closer to the female population norms than to the male population norms.

Francis[40] used the Revised Eysenck Personality Questionnaire[41] among 92 male and 20 female Anglican clergy attending two residential clergy schools. No differences were found for the lie scale or neuroticism scale between the men and women. The female clergy recorded higher scores than the male clergy on the extraversion and psychoticism scales. The results on each of the four scales were contrary to the differences between men and women demonstrated by the population norms.

Canada

Stevens[42] conducted a survey among ordained Anglican women in Canada. A postal questionnaire was sent to all but five of the total number of clergywomen in the Anglican church in Canada. A response rate of 60% (N=108) was achieved. The remaining five clergywomen were interviewed. Stevens employed Gilligan's *different voice* hypotheses[43] as the methodology against which to interpret the results. Gilligan questioned the validity of traditional psychological tests and models when applied to women. Focusing on the work of Kohlberg,[44] she argued that his model of moral development had been designed through studying men, and the assumption that the tests could equally be applied to women was fundamentally flawed. The basis for Gilligan's conclusion was that women respond in a different way or in *a different voice*. Stevens found that the clergywomen in his sample confirmed this hypothesis in respect of their way of relating to others in their ministry.

Conclusions

Four main strands emerge from the group of studies concerned with clergywomen and their ministry. The first strand identified demographics such as age, marital status and educational attainment. The second strand identified that perceptions of levels of support affect clergywomen's ministry. The third strand identified that clergywomen tend to prefer a more collaborative style of leadership. The fourth strand identified aspects of ministry which can be attributed to status and/or a feeling of being valued for the job which they do, such as rates of pay, position(s) held, and perceived progress in the ministerial career path.

Three main strands emerge from the group of studies concerned with clergywomen and their congregation. The first strand, based on contact theory, identified that contact with a clergywoman is usually a positive experience for the laity. However, this acceptance of one individual is not necessarily carried forward to acceptance of clergywomen as a group, although support for the individual may be strong. The second strand, based on organisational maintenance theory, identified that conflict in a congregation is to be avoided and that the appointment of a women is potentially viewed as a source of conflict. The third strand, based on theory concerned with the local/cosmopolitan dichotomy, identified that laity with a conservative, local outlook are more likely to be against clergywomen.

Two main strands emerge from the group of studies concerned with clergywomen as compared with clergymen. The first strand identified that clergywomen tend to experience higher levels of stress. The second strand identified that the ministry of clergywomen and clergymen is more alike than different, although a number of studies have found that there are some differences in ministry style.

Two main strands emerge from the group of studies concerned with psychometric tests. The first strand identified that the BEM Sex Role Inventory demonstrated that clergywomen and clergymen tend to offer a profile that is more alike than theory concerning the differences between men and women would suggest. The second strand identified that, in respect of Eysenck's dimensional model of personality, clergywomen have a more masculine personality profile than clergymen.

Political debate

As well as reflecting on the international research on women in ministry, we wanted our new study to be properly informed by the debate regarding the ordination of women. Our second step, therefore, was to be clear about the implications of the debate going on within the Church of England for the long diaconate.

Although in 1975 the General Synod of the Church of England passed a motion stating that there were 'no fundamental objections to the ordination of women to the priesthood', the formal debate conducted in 1978 failed to remove the legal barriers to the ordination of women as priests.[45] Following the failure of the 1978 debate, three major issues were brought before the General Synod in the subsequent years and passed through the necessary stages of the synodical procedure in relation to women in ordained ministry. The first of these issues led to passing the *Women Ordained Abroad Measure*, the second issue led to passing the *Deacons (the ordination of women) Measure,* and the third issue led to passing the *Priests (ordination of women) Measure.* All three issues are listed by the title given to them in their final form as measures which went before the General Synod.

Women Ordained Abroad Measure

The *Women Ordained Abroad Measure* originated through necessity when the 1978 General Synod failed to remove legal barriers to women being priests. This created a problem for women visiting Britain who had been ordained as priests in other Provinces within the Anglican communion. This growing group of women priests included women like Kath Burn[46] and Elizabeth Canham[47] who had moved abroad in order to seek ordination to the priesthood. The question the Church of England had to resolve was whether to allow visiting women priests from abroad to carry out full priestly duties under license in Britain. This was accepted practice for visiting male priests, as a recognised courtesy.

Accordingly, a standing committee was appointed from the General Synod to consider the issues involved and suggest possible ways by which the situation could be resolved. The report,[48] which put forward seven options, was given for approval to the 1979 General Synod. However, it was decided that, rather than a report, clear legislation was needed which would leave no room for ambiguity with regard to the Church of England's position.

As a consequence, in 1983, the *Draft Women Ordained Abroad Measure*[49] came before the General Synod. Progress was slow, due mainly to a discussion as to whether the legislation came under Article 8.[50] In order that Article 8 could be evoked it had to be agreed that the proposed measure constituted a change in the law. If this was agreed, then the measure would have to go to the dioceses for approval before coming back to the General Synod where it would then require a two thirds majority. Subsequent to a debate and vote, General Synod deemed the measure to be within the scope of Article 8.

Although the measure's passage through General Synod had been viewed as a simple process, it became a political game between those for and those against women priests. Those against women priests seem to have seen their chance to defeat the legislation by placing it under Article 8 business. Opponents at the very least, it seems, were hoping for delay.

In 1984 the measure was passed to the dioceses for discussion and approval or disapproval. The measure was carried by a majority in the dioceses. The way was now clear for the motion to go before General Synod for a final vote. This, the final stage of the *Woman Ordained Abroad Measure*,[51] came before General Synod in 1986. The actual measure in this, its final form, was drawn up in order that women ordained abroad might, after fulfilling certain conditions and provisos, be allowed to conduct all priestly functions within the Church of England under license. By this stage the measure had clearly come to be seen as a vote on the specific principle of women priests, rather than as a measure which would offer the same rights to visiting priests of both sexes.

Deacons (ordination of women) measure

In 1981 a motion was brought before the General Synod by the Bishop of Portsmouth, that the General Synod receive the report *The Deaconess Order and the Diaconate: report by the House of Bishops*.[52] The main focus of the report being 'that the Church of England make provision for, and encourage, men and women to serve in an ordained distinctive diaconate'. The report owed its origins largely to the 1968 Report, *Women in Ministry*.[53] The 1968 report initiated discussions at the 1968 and consequently the 1978 Lambeth Conferences wherein the majority of those present agreed something needed to be done to end the ambiguous position of women within the deaconess movement. These discussions led to the 1981 report which considered the option of opening the diaconate to men and women. This report was accepted and preparation of appropriate legislation commenced via the appointment of a Standing Committee. It was also agreed that representation of deacons at the General Synod should be considered within the scope of the legislation. The Standing Committee brought the report,

The Ordination of Women to the diaconate: report by the Standing Committee[54] before Synod in 1982.

Between 1983 and 1984 the draft measure had been changed in two significant ways. The first way was with regard to matters of doctrine and worship which would need to be changed as a result of the measure. These were to be dealt with by a canon. The reason for this was that, although the *Deacons (ordination of women) Measure* had to pass through parliament, it was felt that parliament should not discuss matters concerning doctrine and worship. The second way was with regard to a clause which was inserted into the measure, clause 1(4), that 'nothing in this measure shall make it lawful for a woman to be ordained to the office of priest'. It was this form of the motion which was sent out to the dioceses. The motion was passed in all but two dioceses, Exeter and Gibraltar in Europe. The motion then returned to General Synod and was passed in 1985. However, it had to return again for approval the following year due to a minor amendment which was suggested by the Parliament's Ecclesiastical Committee. The first women deacons in the Church of England were ordained in 1987.

When women were ordained deacon the problems changed slightly in focus. The ambiguity in the role of the deaconesses was effectively solved as the order was closed to more entrants and women would enter the diaconate. However, much of the ambiguity of the role was now transferred to the diaconate. The diaconate was effectively enlarged to include within it both men and women. At the same time the church had created a permanent diaconate with very little thought as to how it would integrate into the church.

The role of women clergy as permenant deacons tended to be defined in a negative way by what they were *not* allowed to do as compared with a priest. Aldridge[55] summed this issue up: 'The recent decision to ordain women not as deaconesses but as deacons will expand their role only slightly, will not resolve their anomalous status and will merely confirm their subordination to the clergy.' A woman deacon's role in many ways remained as ambiguous as the deaconess role had previously been. Thus, the results were unsatisfactory for all concerned and rather than abating the pressure for women's ordination to the priesthood, as some had hoped, the pressure continued. There is no doubt that a significant number of people did view this decision by the Church of England as the first step toward priesthood for women. Equally there were those who felt that this was far enough for women and that the next step to priesthood for women should never come.

The Ordination of Women to the Priesthood

The debate surrounding the report *The Ordination of Women to the Priesthood*[56] led, in 1975, to two motions being brought before the General Synod of the Church of England. The first motion, 'That this Synod considers that there are no fundamental objections to the ordination of women to the priesthood', was passed. The second motion, containing the necessary legislation to remove the legal barriers to women being priests, failed.

In 1978 the motion to remove legal barriers to women's ordination to the priesthood was brought back to the General Synod to be voted on again. The vote was lost in the House of Clergy. This failure of the motion to remove legal barriers in 1978 acted as the catalyst for the formation of the Movement for the Ordination of Women (MOW).[57]

It was not until 1984 that the issue was raised again in General Synod with the proposal of a motion to initiate the preparation of legislation for the ordination of women to the priesthood. It was brought by the Bishop of Southwark (Ronald Bowlby). Although brought by this one person he was supported by nine dioceses who had sent a clear signal to General Synod by proposing a similar motion. The motion to begin the preparation of legislation was passed. Professor David McClean was appointed chair of the committee to consider the scope of the legislation.

It was from the time of this vote that the two campaigns, the one for and the one against the ordination of women to the priesthood, really began to gather momentum. Organisations were formed to campaign actively against the idea. Three organisations seem to have been of particular importance: The Association for the Apostolic Ministry,[58] Women Against the Ordination of Women (WAOW)[59] and Cost of Conscience.[60] Such groups brought together Anglo-Catholics and Evangelicals, the first focused on the sacraments, the latter the pulpit. Their campaigns, along with MOW, obtained quite a high profile both within and outside the church, pushed forward by the publication of tracts and magazines. In an effort to win support for their respective causes the individual groups enlisted the support of prominent church members including members of parliament.

Further, it was important to both sides to establish who supported them, who did not support them and those who were undecided. It was only by establishing such details that they could grasp how their respective campaigns were progressing. A matter of greater practical importance was ascertaining who among General Synod members supported which point of view and who could be persuaded, as ultimately this was the body who would decide the outcome.

The Ordination of Women to the Priesthood: the scope of the legislation,[61] or the *McClean Report* as it became known, was a disappointment to supporters of women priests when it reported to the General Synod in 1986. This report had seemed to make very little progress, focusing on the needs of those who could not accept women priests rather than actually looking forward to women being priested. It was here, for the first time, that the idea of 'safeguards' was given a prominent position. Due to the obvious problems the committee had faced, a vote was carried by the General Synod to hand the matter over to the House of Bishops who agreed to submit a report in six months. Webster[62] views this as the bishops coming to the rescue.

The bishops produced *The Ordination of Women to the Priesthood: first report by the House of Bishops*[63] in 1987. The bishops divided the report into three main areas: the theological presuppositions, the principles underlying legislation, and the framework for the legislation and safeguards. The underlying concerns of the report were twofold. The first concern questioned whether the ordination of women to the priesthood would be a legitimate development. The second concern questioned whether the ordination of women to the priesthood would constitute a fundamental change. The report provided a useful summary from which the General Synod could work. In this sense it provided a way forward. The report suggested that two separate measures should be drawn up, one to deal with legislation including safeguards and the second to deal with financial provisions. Further, the bishops suggested that matters pertaining to the issue, which were not included in the text of the motion itself, could be included in a *code of practice*. The report was accepted and the preparation of legislation could begin. Professor McClean was given the chair of the Legislative Committee.

In June 1988 the bishops produced a further report dealing in greater detail with the theological issues involved. Gill[64] sees this report as demonstrating that the bishops themselves were clearly not of one mind as there was no relative importance placed on any one of the arguments. However, the draft legislation which would enable women to be priested was approved by General Synod, enabling it to proceed to the revision committee together with proposed financial provisions. The Legislative Committee took the lead from the bishops' report and drafted the necessary legislation in two parts. The first part would effectively remove the legal barriers to women being priests and included the safeguards. The second contained the financial provisions, just as the bishops' report had suggested.

The measures were passed in 1989. It then took a further fifteen months for the legislation to be amended and prepared and passed through General Synod before it could go to the dioceses for approval. The legislation passed to the dioceses in 1990. The motion was carried in thirty eight out of forty four dioceses.

In July 1992, when the General Synod met in York, it became clear, for the first time, just how close the vote was going to be. This led to intense lobbying from the organisations on both sides of the debate. The only thing clear at this stage was that the outcome would be decided by very few votes. This in turn sparked media interest, resulting in television coverage of the debate when it finally took place on 11 November 1992.[65] So many people wanted to speak on the motion presented to the General Synod that speeches had to be kept to an imposed time limit, so that as many people were able to speak as possible. The final form of the measure took its lead from the 1988 bishops' report,[66] in that the first part[67] removed the legal barriers to women becoming priests, while parts two[68] and three[69] dealt with the necessary canons, and part four[70] provided for financial provisions for those clergy who would leave the Church of England should the motion be passed. It was assumed that should the first part of the measure be passed then the rest would follow. This proved to be so when the motion was passed by 39 to 13 in the House of Bishops, 176 to 74 in the House of Clergy and 169 to 82 in the House of Laity, achieving the two thirds majority necessary in each house.

There always seemed to be present the vague idea that when the vote went through everything would quieten down and people would 'get on with the job'; that those who could not accept the decision and decided to the leave the church would be few, and that once they had gone people would pull together. However, this was not to be the case; 'the decision did not bring peace'.[71] There was a brief period of celebration which was rapidly followed by both the church and media focusing on those who could not in conscience accept the decision.

The questionnaire

After reviewing the international research literature and the political debate surrounding the ordination of women to the priesthood in the Church of England, we were able to develop a clearer map of the broad issues with which the questionnaire should be concerned. The next step involved translating this broad map of ideas into groups of sharply focused and concise questions.

One of the key rules of good questionnaire design is that the individual questions should reflect the concerns and language of the group who will be asked to complete it.[72] Interviews provide a good means of access both to the concerns and to the language. Both authors interviewed a number of women deacons before the questionnaire was drafted. Then we discussed initial drafts of the questionnaire with women deacons until we were content that all the essential issues had been covered in ways which were straightforward and in language which was unambiguous.

On the basis of our review of the international research literature, our consideration of the political debate within the Church of England and our interviews with women deacons, the questionnaire was designed to explore the following twenty two key issues which we defined as: call to ministry, selection, first appointment, training incumbent, last appointment as deacon, last incumbent as deacon, clerical colleagues, parishioners, family, friends, collaborative ministry, stress in ministry, satisfaction in ministry, public role, pastoral role, social role, liturgical role, inclusive language, church's attitude to women, ordination debate, the legislation for the ordination of women and implications for relationships with other churches, and the future possibilities including women bishops. These twenty two key issues provide the structure for the main part of this book. Our intention now is to introduce each issue briefly.

Call to ministry

The attempt to understand the long diaconate begins properly with an exploration of how the women deacons perceived their call to ministry. Traditionally Anglicanism has regarded ministry as a vocation having its origin in a call from God, rather than in a call from the congregation, or in a personal choice of career.[73] Against this background we wanted to explore two issues.

The first issue concerns the women deacons' understanding of their vocation and the ways in which they express that understanding. To what extent did the women deacons concur with the view that they had sought ordination to the diaconate in response to a call from God? How conscious were they of seeking ordination as a way of giving greater authority to their ministry? How much did they seek ordination as a deliberate strategy to change the perceived sexist nature of the church?[74]

The second issue concerns the women deacons' perceptions of the difficulties which may have stood in their path of responding to the call. To what extent were the women deacons conscious of their gender standing in the way? How much had they felt inwardly discouraged from seeking ordination? How much had they experienced outward discouragement from others?

Selection

Having identified a call to ordination, the next step on the journey involves having that call tested by the church. Candidates who survive certain screening processes within their own diocese are then referred to the formal selection conference arranged by the Advisory Board of Ministry (ABM), or in earlier days by the Advisory Council for the Church's Ministry (ACCM).[75] We wanted to explore two aspects of this process.

First, the women deacons in the present study are those who survived the selection process. Anecdotal evidence suggests that sometimes even the survivors may feel ambivalent about the process of their selection. To what extent, then, were the women deacons now able to look back on their selection conference as a positive experience, or to what extent did they feel that their experience was a negative one? Did any of them feel disadvantaged in the selection process by their gender?[76]

Second, at their selection conference the women deacons will have been interviewed by and worked with a small group of trained selectors whose role was to test their vocation in depth and with thoroughness.[77] What did these women deacons make of the selectors themselves? Did they feel that the selectors treated them fairly and in a friendly manner? Did any of them feel that the selectors had failed to take them seriously or treated them in a hostile or patronising way?

First appointment

Initial clergy training is generally considered to involve two stages: a period at a theological college or on a ministry training course, followed by a first curacy under the guidance of a 'training incumbent'.[78] The experience of ordinands at theological colleges or on ministry training courses is a crucial area of study in its own right.[79] In order to focus more closely on the experiences of ministry we decided to ask no questions about the time spent at college or on a course. We move, therefore, directly from selection to the first appointment.

The first appointment in the training parish can be of fundamental importance to both male and female clergy in shaping their future attitude toward ministry and in developing their practical skills in ministry.[80] Much may depend on the ways in which training incumbents feel willing or able to share the responsibilities of ministry with their new and junior colleagues.

In particular we wanted to examine how much responsibility the women deacons felt they had really been allowed to share in their training parish. How many felt properly included in making parish decisions? How many women deacons felt exploited by having too much work delegated to them? Or how many felt that insufficient use had been made of their talents, or that too little had been asked of them? To what extent did the women deacons feel that they had been properly supported by adequate feedback during their training period in the parish?

Training incumbent

Often the key to the success of the first appointment rests in the quality of the relationship between the curate and the training incumbent. Recognition of the importance of this relationship is reflected in the increasing attention given by the Anglican church to the proper selection and training of training incumbents.[81]

The ordination of women to the diaconate introduced a crucial new factor, however, to the relationship between curate and training incumbent, previously uncomplicated by gender differences. Moreover, as long as the Church of England accepted women in the order of deacon, but not in the order of priest, newly ordained women deacons invariably found themselves assigned to a male priest as training incumbent. Many male priests may have found themselves inadequately prepared for the inevitable change in relational dynamics when they received their first women deacons as curate. In this context we wanted to explore two specific issues.

The first issue concerned how much women deacons perceived their relationship with their training incumbent to have been adversely influenced by the difference in gender. How many of the women deacons felt that their training incumbent was uncomfortable working with a female colleague? To what extent did the women deacons perceive their training incumbent to have been over protective, or generally unhelpful?

The second issue concerned the extent to which the close working relationship between male training incumbent and female curate could also introduce new suspicions and strains on existing personal relationships. How many women deacons felt that their partner experienced the training incumbent as a threat? Or how many felt that their training incumbent's wife experienced them as a threat?

Last appointment as deacon

By January 1994 many men deaconed in 1987 and priested in 1988 would have moved into their first incumbency and assumed the responsibilities of sole pastoral charge. Such opportunities were rarely open to women in deacons' orders. Consequently the woman deacon who wished to remain in parish ministry after serving her training curacy would still be responsible to a male incumbent, continuing to work either as a senior assistant curate, as a parish deacon, or as a member of a team ministry. Very few had attained the status of deacon-in-charge.[82] In this context we wanted to explore the extent to which frustrations experienced during the training curacy extended into the later phase of ministry, by asking similar questions regarding their last appointment as deacon to those asked regarding their first appointment.

For example, how many women in their last appointment as deacon felt properly included in making decisions in their parishes, or in having a fair share of responsibility in parish ministry? How many women in their last appointment as deacon felt that their incumbent failed to delegate sufficient aspects of ministry to them? Or how many felt exploited by having too much work delegated to them? To what extent did they feel that sufficient use was being made of their talents? To what extent did they feel that they were being supported by adequate feedback?

Last incumbent as deacon

For their last appointment as deacon, the quality of the working relationship with the incumbent is probably as important as it was during the training curacy. There is, however, one very important difference at this later stage of ministry. The women deacons may have had considerably greater opportunity to choose with whom they worked in subsequent appointments than was the case in their initial appointment. Against this background we wanted to explore two issues.

The first issue concerned whether the women deacons perceived their relationship with their last incumbent as deacon to have been different from their relationship with their training incumbent. How many of the women deacons felt that their last incumbent, while they remained in deacon's orders, was generally unhelpful or unconstructive toward them? Or how many felt that their last incumbent, while they remained in deacon's orders, was uncomfortable working with a female colleague?

The second issue concerned the impact of the working relationship between female curate, female team vicar or female parish deacon and male incumbent on other personal relationships. At this stage of their ministry, how many women deacons felt they were perceived as a threat by their incumbent's wife? Or how many felt that their own partner perceived their incumbent as a threat?

Clerical colleagues

While it is likely that the majority of women deacons would have been placed with incumbents who had at least some sympathy for the ministry of women, there could be little guarantee that the wider contexts of the deanery, archdeanery and diocese in which they were located would be so sympathetic. For example, clergy chapters had been constituted as organisations for men only for a number of years and anecdotal evidence pointed to occasions when these chapters strenuously resisted the proper integration of women. We wished, therefore, to explore how the women deacons experienced their reception by their clerical colleagues.

For example, how much did the women deacons really feel part of the professional life of other clergy in their area? To what extent did they experience trouble with some of their colleagues? How many of the women deacons were conscious of their clerical colleagues being unhappy when they took up their last appointment as deacon specifically because they were women? To what extent did they sense that their clerical colleagues' attitude toward women in ministry changed as a result of their own ministry in the area?

Parishioners

The question of the ordination of women caused division not only between parishes but within parishes. While some congregations may have positively sought women deacons, other congregations may have clearly refused receiving women deacons. Inevitably some congregations were divided internally on this issue and women deacons will have been placed in churches where their ministry may have been unacceptable to some.[83] In this context we wanted to explore two issues.

The first issue concerned the extent to which women deacons found themselves working in churches where the ministry of women was fully acceptable, and the extent to which women deacons experienced a lack of acceptance from the congregation. Overall, how supportive did the women deacons find their congregation? How much did they feel appreciated? How well did they feel accepted?

The second issue concerned the way in which this first generation of women working in an *ordained* capacity within the Church of England witnessed changes in the attitudes of their congregations as a consequence of their ministry. To what extent did they experience congregations becoming more favourable to women in ministry, or to what extent did they experience attitudes becoming more hardened against women in ministry?

Family

Like the majority of male clergy, many women deacons combine their professional commitment to the church with marriage and family life. Changes both in society as a whole and in the church seem to be placing clergy marriages under increasing pressure.[84] It is unlikely that the family pressures documented among male clergy have also been extended to female clergy. We wanted, therefore, to give particular attention to how married women deacons evaluated the effect of ministry on their family life.

First, we recognised that there could be a clear danger for some married women deacons that the demands of ministry might encroach over the whole of life. What proportion of the married women deacons found that they often did not have enough time for their family? Or what proportion of married women deacons found their partners resentful of the amount of time they spent in ministry?

Second, we recognised that historically there had been the expectation that married Anglican priests were supported in their ministry by their wives. To what extent had this image now been transferred to the husbands of the married women deacons? What proportion of married women deacons found their partner supportive of their ministry? How many married women deacons found that their partner took an active interest in their ministry?

Friends

The demands of ordained life carry all kinds of implications for friendship patterns. At one level, the ordained clergy are welcomed into the ready made friendship networks of their local church. They may be surrounded by potential friends. At another level, the ordained clergy are expected to maintain a proper professional distance and objectivity within the life of the local church. They may as a consequence remain lonely and isolated. Clergy who are reluctant to invest heavily in friendships within their parish may rely on friendships established before ordination or during their period of training. The problem is that a busy and mobile career may make the sustaining of such friendships increasingly difficult.[85] Against this background we wished to explore two issues.

The first issue concerned the relationship between personal life and professional life. To what extent did the women deacons find that they had kept a clear separation between private life and ministerial duties? How difficult had it been for them to make friends with people in the parish?

The second issue concerned the maintenance of friendships outside the parish. To what extent did the women deacons look outside the parish for their close friends? Or to what extent were they still drawing on the pattern of friendships established prior to ordination?

Collaborative ministry

A number of commentators on the ministry style exercised by women suggest that women deacons may prefer a more collaborative style of ministry than that exercised by clergymen.[86] We were interested to test, therefore, the extent to which the women deacons were conscious of involving others in their ministry. For example, how much did they feel that they took other people's views fully into account in shaping their ministry? To what extent did they find that it came naturally to delegate responsibilities to others?

We also recognised that a collaborative style of ministry carried certain hidden costs. Those who wish to encourage collaboration may find themselves trying too hard to accommodate other people's points of view. We were interested to test, therefore, the extent to which the women deacons were conscious of coming under pressure from others. For example, how much did they feel that other people were trying too hard to influence their ministry? To what extent did they feel that other people interfered too much in their ministry?

Stress in ministry

A number of recent studies have drawn attention to the growing problems of stress and burnout in ministry.[87] Clergy stress has negative consequences not only for the individual clergy, but also for their families and their parishioners. While it was not possible within the scope of the present survey to concentrate adequately on the assessment of stress levels among the women deacons, we wished to be able to include some markers of sources of stress, signs of stress, and consequences of stress.

A major source of stress in ministry arises from setting unrealistic and unattainable expectations. To what extent were the women deacons conscious of imposing unrealistic expectations on themselves? For women deacons another source of stress might be traced to the very nature of diaconal ministry, when the diaconate did not lead into priesthood. To what extent did these women deacons feel constrained by the limits of their ministry position?

A major sign of stress in ministry occurs when ministry begins to take over the whole of life. To what extent were the women deacons conscious of no longer having time for their hobbies and interests? Or to what extent were they conscious of simply not having enough time for themselves?

A major consequence of stress is reflected in feelings of isolation and loneliness. To what extent were the women deacons conscious of feeling lonely and isolated in their ministry?

Satisfaction in ministry

Recent strands of research on professional burnout make a clear distinction between the assessment of stress and the assessment of satisfaction.[88] To experience stress in ministry does not necessarily imply a lack of personal satisfaction from ministry. Indeed, sometimes high levels of stress and high levels of personal satisfaction can go hand in hand.

Consequently, we wished to include in the survey a range of markers concerned with satisfaction in ministry.

Satisfaction can derive from the sense that something worthwhile is being accomplished. What proportion of the women deacons felt that they were really accomplishing things in their ministry?

Satisfaction can derive from the sense that difficulties are being overcome and solutions are being found to problems. What proportion of the women deacons felt that they were really successful at overcoming difficulties in their ministry?

Satisfaction can derive from the sense of personal growth and development. What proportion of the women deacons felt that they were really growing spiritually in their ministry?

Satisfaction can be derived from being able to live without undue financial anxiety and worry about money. What proportion of the women deacons felt satisfied that they had enough money to life comfortably?

Public role

A number of commentators on women in ministry argue that, by the very nature of being female, clergywomen bring different skills to ministry from those skills brought by clergymen and that, as a consequence, they express their ministry differently from the way in which ministry is expressed by men.[89] Some exponents of this view take a somewhat stronger line and argue that this difference is in fact a sign of superiority. Women clergy, they argue, are better at some aspects of ministry than male clergy.[90] This section and the following three sections were concerned to examine the extent to which the women deacons perceived women clergy to be better than male clergy in specific areas of ministry. We examined this issue by distinguishing between four different areas of ministry.[91]

The first area of ministry concerned the public role of the clergy. Examples of the public role of the clergy include visiting people in their homes, visiting people in hospital, acting as teachers, working as evangelists, or becoming leaders in the local community.[92] Some of these functions may need the ability to stand out in the crowd or to take the lead on a public occasion. Others of these functions may need a high level of interpersonal skill and empathy. Some people, for example, might argue that women deacons would see themselves as having particular skills to offer in areas like hospital visiting, and consequently make a better job of that aspect of ministry than male clergy. Conversely, women deacons might see themselves as less well equipped for areas like becoming leaders in the local community, and consequently make a less satisfactory job of this aspect of ministry than male clergy. The survey allows these theories to be tested.

Pastoral role

The second area of ministry concerns the pastoral role of the clergy. Examples of the pastoral role of the clergy include baptism preparation, confirmation preparation, marriage preparation, marital counselling and spiritual direction.[93] Many of these functions involve working closely and sensitively alongside individuals at important times in their lives. Some people might argue that women are better than men at developing interpersonal skills in such contexts, and perhaps especially at times of bereavement. Others, however, would want to reject such cultural stereotypes. Once again, the survey allows these theories to be tested.

Social role

The third area of ministry concerns the social role of the clergy. For example, there are expectations that clergy should be competent to work among different age categories of young people. Many churches operate parent and toddler groups or play groups which expect clergy to work successfully among pre-schoolers. Many churches promote contact with local primary schools, either because they are church foundations or because county schools welcome links with the wider community. Such contacts expect clergy to work successfully among primary school children. Many churches expect clergy to work successfully among teenagers, often by visiting local secondary schools or through youth groups.[94]

On a rather different front, many churches run groups for women, like the Mother's Union. A smaller number of churches run groups exclusively for men. Clergy are expected to work successfully in single sex groups of adults as well as in mixed groups.

Some people might argue that women clergy are better than male clergy at working with pre-schoolers, primary school children and women, while male clergy are better than women clergy at working with teenagers and men. Others, however, would want to reject such cultural stereotypes. Once again, the survey allows these theories to be tested.

Liturgical role

The third area of ministry concerns the liturgical role of the clergy. On the one hand, there are important distinctions between the liturgical functions of deacons and priests.[95] While priests can preside at the eucharist, deacons cannot do so. On the other hand, there are many liturgical functions which can be performed equally by deacons and by priests. Both can lead public worship and conduct the statutory services of matins and evensong. Both can preach. Both can be involved in the occasional offices of baptisms, weddings and funerals.[96]

Some might argue that the pastoral sensitivity of women clergy would equip them especially well for their liturgical function at funerals. Others, however, would want to reject such cultural stereotypes. Once again, the survey allows these theories to be tested.

Inclusive language

Masculine imagery and masculine language have long been engrained within the theology and liturgy of the Church of England. The case for inclusive language was ignored by the *Alternative Service Book 1980* and has continued to be ignored by many new hymn books and many new bible translations. Inclusive language was by no means an established feature of the church into which women were first ordained deacon in 1987.[97] While some male clergy within the Church of England appeared to have become increasingly conscious of sexist language by the end of the 1980s, it may be anticipated that women deacons would be particularly aware of the incongruity between their own gender and the language frequently promoted in church. Against this background, we wanted to explore three issues.

The first issue concerned the attitude of the women deacons to the use of inclusive language. What proportion of the women deacons considered that inclusive language should be used in service books, in bible translations, or in hymns?

The second issue concerned the sensitivity of the women deacons to the controversial nature of inclusive language in churches. What proportion of the women deacons considered that the use of inclusive language would be controversial in most congregations?

The third issue took one step beyond inclusive language to assess the views of the women deacons on the use of female imagery for God alongside the well established use of male imagery for God. What proportion of the women deacons considered that hymns and prayers should use female imagery for God?

Church's attitude to women

Women ordained to the diaconate in the Church of England between 1987 and 1992 entered ministry in a church which remained fundamentally unsure about the ordination of women to the priesthood. We wanted to know what kind of messages were being communicated to the women deacons by the situation.[98] In this connection we focused on two kinds of question.

The first question concerned the women deacons' interpretation of the church's attitude toward women. To what extent did they feel that the Church of England did not actively encourage women to ordained ministry? Or, having been ordained, how many of them felt that the Church of England discouraged women deacons from applying for jobs with a high profile? How many of them felt that the Church of England's attitude to women deacons challenged their vocation or made them question their own calling?

The second question concerned the way in which the Church of England's attitude toward the ordination of women may have made difficulties for women deacons in some areas of their work. To what extent did the women deacons feel this to be the case, especially as this affected their work with men and with women differently?

Ordination debate

At the time when the survey was underway, the implications of the debate regarding the ordination of women to the priesthood were being widely discussed both within the church and by the media.[99] While some within the church were now preparing carefully for the first services to ordain women to the priesthood, others were actively trying to challenge the decision of the General Synod or making plans to leave the Church of England.[100] The whole controversy continued to be given a high profile by the religious and secular press. We wanted to know what impact this debate was having on the women deacons themselves, with special reference to two issues.

The first issue concerned the impact of the media. To what extent did the women deacons feel that the media was treating the debate fairly, or did they suspect that the media's attention was focused too heavily on the opponents to women priests? More generally, did the women deacons feel that the media's attention was detrimental to the image of the church?

The second issue concerned the attitude of the women deacons to the opponents to the ordination of women to the priesthood. How much did the women deacons try to understand the viewpoint of those who could not accept the ordination of women? How accepting were they of those who took that position?

Legislation and ecumenism

When the General Synod passed the *Priests (ordination of women) Measure*, this legislation signalled that at last an end was in sight for the long diaconate. The legislation also signalled a somewhat wider range of new possibilities and a number of new problems to be confronted by the Church of England. In this context we wanted to examine three issues.

The first issue concerned the personal response of the women deacons to the positive outcome of the debate in the General Synod. What did this outcome do for the women deacons' own sense of ministry and vocation?

The second issue concerned the way in which the women deacons regarded the safeguards imposed by the measure to protect the position of those who remained unhappy with the Church of England ordaining women to the priesthood. These safeguards made financial provisions for those clergymen who no longer felt able to function as priest within the Church of England.[101] To what extent did the women deacons regard these safeguards as acceptable measures? Or to what extent did they perceive these safeguards as discriminatory against women?

The third issue concerns the way in which the women deacons perceived the implications of the *Priests (ordination of women) Measure* for the relationship between the Church of

England and other churches in Britain which already ordained women, with other Provinces of the Anglican communion, and with the Roman Catholic Church.[102]

Bishops and beyond

Passing the *Priests (ordination of women) Measure* may have been an important milestone in the recognition of the ministry of women within the Church of England by drawing to a close the long diaconate, but this is by no means the end of the journey. We wanted, therefore, to close the survey by assessing how the women deacons perceived the way ahead. In particular we wanted to explore two specific issues.

The first issue concerned the appointment of women clergy to senior positions in the church. Once ordained to the priesthood, how keen were the women deacons to see women clergy appointed to senior positions in the church? Then, how much do they envisage that the appointment of women clergy to senior positions in the church will be a cause of further controversy?

The second issue concerned the consecration of women as bishops within the Church of England.[103] How willing were the women deacons to support the idea of women being appointed as bishops? And do they really think that women are likely to be consecrated as bishops in the Church of England within the near future?

The Survey

Once agreement had been reached about the twenty two key issues to be covered by the questionnaire, a small set of items was selected to sample the content of each issue. Each set contained no fewer than five items and no more than nine items.

In selecting these items we followed the general principles of item construction recommended in social research. Each item had to be short, clear, unambiguous and containing no more than one idea.[104]

Questionnaire design

A variety of different techniques exists for recording or scaling responses to questionnaire items. Often market surveys simply invite those completing the questionnaire to tick the statement with which they agree. The problem with the method is that it is impossible to know whether the respondent actually disagrees with those items which are not ticked or has simply overlooked them. A slightly more sophisticated technique places the two options 'yes' and 'no' by each statement and the respondent is asked to select one or the other.[105] The problem with this approach is that some respondents are genuinely unable to be so decisive about every issue. The third technique provides a range of three options: 'yes', 'no' and 'uncertain' in order to recognise that the 'uncertain' response is appropriate and valid.[106]

Back in the 1930s a fourth technique was introduced to recording or scaling responses to questionnaire items by R.A. Likert, in order to allow a greater degree of tone and precision to be achieved.[107] What has subsequently become known as *Likert scaling* generally invites respondents to assess each statement on a five point continuum. The five points are generally defined as 'agree strongly', 'agree', 'not certain', 'disagree' and 'disagree strongly'. We decided to adopt the Likert scaling technique, having found it to be useful in a number of previous studies.

In addition to the central section of our questionnaire using the Likert scaling technique, the questionnaire included three other main sections. The first section used mainly multiple choice questions, together with a few open ended questions in order to provide a detailed profile of the background of each woman deacon who took part in the survey. This part of the questionnaire provided information about such issues as schooling and work experience prior to ordination. The third section of the questionnaire presented the short form Revised Eysenck Personality Questionnaire.[108] This instrument provided scores for each of the women deacons on the three major personality dimensions of extraversion, neuroticism and psychoticism. It also contained a lie scale to help identify those who wished to present themselves in a favourable but unrealistic light. The fourth section of the questionnaire presented an inventory concerned with clergy roles and role expectations. This inventory had been used in an earlier study among men.[109]

The Long Diaconate is based almost entirely on the information provided by the first and second part of the questionnaire. The results from the personality questionnaire have already begun to emerge in other publications.[110] We hope to begin work on analysing and interpreting the fourth part of the questionnaire shortly.

When finally organised and printed, the questionnaire was presented as a twenty eight page booklet.

Distribution

The Church Commissioners kindly provided us with a printout of all women deacons licensed in the Anglican church in England, Ireland, Wales and Scotland, up to and including the age of seventy, whether in stipendiary or non-stipendiary ministry. The questionnaires were mailed together with a covering letter and a freepost reply envelope.

The covering letter explained the purposes of the survey and guaranteed confidentiality and anonymity. It also explained that the questionnaire carried an identification number in order to help us send reminders to those who did not reply. Once the questionnaire had been returned to us we removed the number so that no further link could be made to the individual who had completed it.

The Church Commissioners' data base had identified 1,795 names and addresses. Inevitably some of the addresses were no longer up to date or were inaccurate in one way or another. As a consequence of this 97 envelopes were returned to us by the Post Office as undeliverable, reducing the total number of questionnaires delivered to 1,698.

Over the course of the next months two further letters were sent to those who had not initially responded by completing the questionnaire. Then telephone calls were made. Eventually a total of 1,239 thoroughly completed questionnaires were returned to us, as well as some further questionnaires which were only partially completed. We decided only to include in our analyses the questionnaires which had been filled in completely. This means that we are reporting on a response rate of 73%.[111]

By general standards of postal questionnaires our response rate is excellent and may be taken as an indication of the seriousness with which the women deacons took our survey. We are grateful to each one who took the time and trouble to help us.

For *The Long Diaconate* we are looking only at the women deacons within the Church of England. Since many features of the situations in Ireland, Scotland and Wales are different from the situation in England, it seemed sensible to concentrate on one clearly defined group. Other aspects of our research have made use of data from all four countries. We have previously published a detailed profile of the women deacons within the Church in Wales.[112] Of the 1,239 questionnaires returned to us, 1,139 were from women deacons serving in the Church of England. It is these 1,139 women deacons on whom *The Long Diaconate* is based.

The women deacons

Information provided in the first part of the questionnaire enables us to build up an overall profile of the women deacons serving in the Church of England immediately prior to the first ordinations of women to the priesthood.

Age

At the time of the survey, the majority of the women deacons were in their forties or fifties. The four youngest respondents were twenty six years of age, while the six eldest respondents were seventy one years of age. While the mailing list of those to whom the questionnaires had been sent included women deacons only up to the age of seventy, we had expected a few to have celebrated their seventy first birthday between the time when the mailing list had been generated and the time when they completed the questionnaire.

All told, therefore, 2% of the women deacons were in their twenties, 19% in their thirties, 32% in their forties, 31% in their fifties, 14% in their sixties and 2% were aged seventy or seventy one.

Marital status

At the time of the survey, the majority of women deacons were or had been married. Thus, 55% were currently married, including 1% who had been divorced and remarried. A further 5% were widowed, 5% were divorced and not remarried, and less than 1% were separated. The remaining 34% were single.

Looked at from another perspective, 44% of the women deacons lived without a partner, 54% were living with a male partner and 2% were living with a female partner.

Of the partner with whom the women deacons were living, 73% were in full-time employment, 6% were in part-time employment, 4% were unemployed, and 17% were retired.

Almost one in five of the women deacons (19%) were married to an Anglican priest.

Form of ministry

A higher proportion of the women deacons were received into stipendiary ministry (62%) than into non-stipendiary ministry

(38%). Some of those who entered stipendiary ministry were in fact going into part-time positions, while some of those who entered non-stipendiary ministry were regarding themselves as exercising that ministry full-time. The picture for the total sample of 1,139 women deacons was as follows. For 55% their first appointment as deacon was to full-time stipendiary ministry, for 7% to part-time stipendiary ministry, for 11% to full-time non-stipendiary ministry, and for 27% to part-time non-stipendiary ministry.

For the majority of women deacons (94%) their first appointment had been parochially related. Of those ordained into parochial ministry, 16% were located in rural parishes, 9% in market towns, 14% in small towns, 14% in large towns, 18% in inner city parishes, and 28% in suburban parishes.

By the time that they completed the survey, the proportion of women deacons who regarded themselves as primarily in parochial ministry had fallen to 76%. Of the total sample, 50% now regarded themselves as primarily in stipendiary parochial ministry, while 26% regarded themselves as primarily in non-stipendiary parochial ministry. Of the remaining quarter of the women deacons, 12% regarded themselves as primarily in stipendiary non-parochial ministry and 4% in non-stipendiary non-parochial ministry. A further 3% were retired, another 3% had transferred entirely to secular employment and the remaining 1% regarded themselves as unemployed.

Religious background

The majority of the women deacons had grown up in a religiously active environment. Just one in ten (11%) had not grown up feeling that they belonged to a Christian denomination. Between two thirds and three quarters (71%) had grown up as Anglicans, 5% as Methodists, 3% as Presbyterians or members of the United Reformed Church, 3% as Baptists, 2% as Roman Catholics, 1% as Congregationalists and 1% as Brethren. A small number of the women deacons had their roots in the Assemblies of God, the House Churches, the Lutheran Church, the Orthodox Church and the Salvation Army. One had converted to Anglicanism from the Jewish faith.

During their years at primary school, nearly two thirds (63%) of the women deacons had been weekly church goers, while only 11% never attended church at that stage of their lives. The remaining 26% attended church, but not as often as weekly. During their years at secondary school the proportion of the women deacons who attended church weekly grew to nearly three quarters (73%). By this time only 6% never attended church, while the remaining 21% attended church, but not as often as weekly.

During their school years over three quarters of the women deacons were supported by church going mothers. For 42% of the women deacons, their mothers attended church weekly, while for 7% their mothers attended church at least monthly. A further 28% of mothers attended church occasionally, leaving only 23% who never attended.

Although men are generally less likely to attend church than women,[113] over three fifths of the women deacons were supported by church going fathers during their school years. For 34% of the women deacons, their fathers attended church weekly, while for 5% their fathers attended church at least monthly. A further 21% of fathers attended church occasionally, leaving only 21% who never attended.

Educational background

Quite a high proportion of the women deacons had received schooling outside the state maintained system. Just over a quarter (27%) had received all or part of their primary education in the independent sector, while an equal proportion (27%) had received all or part of their secondary education in the independent sector.

After school and prior to ministry training three fifths of the women deacons (62%) had graduated from higher education. Thus, 51% had earned a first degree, 8% a masters degree and 3% a doctorate.

Employment background

The majority of women deacons had experience of secular employment before entering ministry. A detailed analysis of the kinds of jobs which they had held demonstrates the wide and varied experiences and skills which these women deacons brought to their ministry. Two out of every five (40%) of the women deacons who had experience of secular employment before entering ministry gained this experience as school teachers. The remaining 60% were split between 98 different occupations. These included secretaries, shopworkers, nurses, accountants, computer programmers, pharmacists, farmers, policewomen, bar maids and vets.

Immediately prior to being made deacon, many of the women deacons had served in the order of deaconess.

Church tradition

The questionnaire included two markers to profile the church tradition with which the women deacons identified. Both were defined as seven point semantic differential grids.[114] The first grid was anchored by the contrasting terms *Catholic* and *Evangelical*. The second grid was anchored by the contrasting terms *Liberal* and *Conservative*. The women deacons were asked to circle one number between each pair of descriptors.

The responses demonstrate that 26% of the women deacons identified themselves as Evangelicals, while 19% identified themselves as Catholics. The remaining 55% opted for three middle points on the continuum. At the same time, 18% of the women deacons identified themselves as conservatives, while 25% identified themselves as liberals. The remaining 57% opted for three middle points on the continuum.

The higher proportion of women deacons describing themselves as Evangelicals compared with those describing themselves as Catholics is reflected in the theological colleges or ministry training course on which they trained. The colleges which had trained at least forty five of the women deacons were: Lincoln, Oak Hill Theological College, Salisbury and Wells, St John's Durham, St John's Nottingham, The Queen's College at Birmingham and Trinity College Bristol.

Satisfaction in ministry

Overall the majority of the women deacons presented themselves as happy in ordained ministry. For example, only 13% reported that they were dissatisfied with their present appointment, compared with 87% who were satisfied with their present appointment. Two thirds (67%) had never considered leaving ministry since their ordination, while 21% had thought about leaving once or twice and 12% had thought about leaving more frequently. Around 14% had made enquiries about or applications for other forms of employment.

Future plans

Since the survey was conducted a short while before the first ordinations of women to the priesthood, the first part of the questionnaire ended by testing the intentions of these women deacons to seek ordination to the priesthood. Nearly nine in every ten (88%) were clear that they would do so as soon as possible; 3% wished to delay for a while before seeking priesting; 5% were not clear whether they wished to go forward to priesting or not and the remaining 3% were clear that they would not seek ordination to the priesthood.

The analysis

The second and major part of the questionnaire was designed to provide information about twenty two key issues relevant to understanding the views of women deacons within the Church of England toward the end of the long diaconate. Having organised this information in a relatively sophisticated way through the use of Likert scaling, all kinds of statistical analysis are open to us. In some of our presentations in the scientific journals we have been particularly interested in exploring the cumulative scaling properties of item sets and modelling the cumulative scale scores by means of path analysis and multiple regression. Our aim in *The Long Diaconate*, however, is to present the fruits of the research in a way much more accessible to a non-scientific readership. The most sophisticated statistic we shall employ, therefore, is the simple percentage. Our aim, then, is to *describe* our data and to offer some reflection on that description. Often the description and reflection may raise new questions which subsequent and more sophisticated analyses will be able to check. This kind of analysis, however, is better placed in the academic journals concerned with the scientific study of religion, empirical theology, or the pastoral sciences.

Overview

In each chapter the presentation of the data begins with an overview, considering the 1,239 women deacons together as one group. In the overview the statistics are presented in a table, using three columns. The first column brings together those who checked either the 'agree' or the 'agree strongly' categories on the questionnaire. The second column presents those who checked the 'not certain' category on the questionnaire. The third column brings together those who checked either the 'disagree' or the 'disagree strongly' categories on the questionnaire. In each case the percentage figures have been rounded to the nearest whole number. The consequence of such rounding is that, while the majority of the rows add up precisely to 100%, some rows may add up to either 99% or 101%. Following the overview each chapter then cross tabulates the data by four key variables.

Does age make a difference?

The first comparison examines the relationship between the women deacons' responses to the questions and their ages by dividing the total sample of 1,139 into four age groups. All told, 235 of the women deacons were under the age of forty, 360 were in their forties, 358 were in their fifties, and 185 were between the ages of sixty and seventy one. The sample did not include women deacons over the age of seventy one.

We were interested in exploring possible age differences in the views of the women deacons because research conducted among other groups of clergy and in other cultures has tended to draw attention to significant differences in attitudes and beliefs among different cohorts.[115] For example, Alan Aldridge's survey draws attention to the relation between age and clergy attitudes to liturgical change.[116]

Does marital status make a difference?

The second comparison examines the relationship between the women deacons' responses to the questions and their marital status by dividing the total sample of 1,139 into four groups. All told, 34% of the women deacons were single, 55% were married, 5% were widowed, 5% were divorced and 1% were divorced and remarried. For the purposes of this analysis women deacons living with same sex partners were categorised with the single. Those who were widowed or divorced *and* remarried were categorised with the married.

We were interested in exploring possible differences in the views of the women deacons according to marital status because marital status has been strangely overlooked as a predictor of attitudes in many studies of clergy.[117]

Does church tradition make a difference?

The third comparison examines the relationship between the women deacons' responses to the questions and their church tradition by dividing the total sample of 1,139 into three groups. In the questionnaire the women deacons had been invited to identify their church tradition on a seven point scale, where 1 was anchored as Catholic and 7 was anchored as Evangelical. In this analysis the 19% of women who had selected 1 or 2 on the seven point scale were styled 'Catholic'. The 25% of women who had selected 6 or 7 on the seven point scale were styled 'Evangelical'. The 55% of women who had selected 3, 4 or 5 on the seven point scale were styled 'middle way Anglicans'.

Historically church tradition has played a key role in shaping the Church of England as we know it today. Both the Catholic wing[118] and the Evangelical wing[119] established theological colleges during the mid nineteenth century and some of these colleges continue to train clergy today within the framework of their specific tradition. The middle way of Anglicanism represents the broad church standing between the two distinctive wings.[120]

We were interested in exploring possible differences in the views of the women deacons according to church traditions because several strands of recent research concerned with the Church of England have continued to demonstrate the power of church tradition to shape significant differences in aspects of church life. For example, in their two studies *In the Catholic Way*[121] and *In the Evangelical Way,*[122] Leslie J. Francis and David W. Lankshear demonstrate how churches associated with these two traditions continue to have different attitudes toward issues like the age of confirmation and the seriousness with which they take work among teenagers. In another study Leslie J. Francis and Hugh Thomas explored the differences in the personality profiles of Anglo-Catholic and Evangelical male priests.[123]

Are non-stipendiaries different?

The fourth comparison examines the relationship between the women deacons' responses to the questions and the kind of ministry in which they were engaged by dividing the total sample of 1,139 into two groups. The first group comprised the stipendiary women deacons who regarded the primary focus of their ministry to be parish based. The second group comprised the non-stipendiary women deacons who regarded the primary focus of their ministry to be parish based. This analysis, therefore, excluded both the stipendiary women deacons and the non-stipendiary women deacons who see their ministry essentially in non-parochial terms. This decision guaranteed that when we made comparisons between stipendiary and non-stipendiary women deacons we were looking at individuals who shared at least certain commitments and experiences in common. As a consequence we could attribute differences identified in our analysis with more confidence to the issue of stipendiary versus non-stipendiary ministry rather than to other ways in which the two groups may have differed.

We were interested in exploring possible differences in the views of stipendiary women deacons and non-stipendiary women deacons because the potentially important differences between these two forms of ministry have been largely ignored by empirical research.[124]

Hearing the stories

As well as providing statistics, the questionnaire also included spaces for qualitative data where the women deacons could write in open ended responses and amplify their answers to the pre-coded statements. Each chapter ends by drawing on their open ended responses in order to help us listen to the stories and to the perspectives of individual women deacons. Each extract presented in this section is identified by the writers' age and form of ministry, although the writer herself remains strictly anonymous.

1 Call to ministry

Introduction

The clerical profession is generally regarded as a vocation in at least two senses of the word. In a popular sense the church's ministry is regarded as a vocation alongside careers like nursing and teaching. Practitioners are thought to enter such professions from a sense of commitment to the welfare of others rather than from a desire for wealth or social status. In a theological sense the church's ministry is regarded as a vocation in a somewhat different way. Clergy are thought to be called by God to serve in the church's ministry rather than choosing that career for themselves. Their vocation is literally the response to a call.

This chapter sets out to explore how women deacons experienced the call to ordained ministry. In particular the chapter examines two main issues. The first issue concerns the way in which women deacons expressed their understanding of vocation. To what extent were women deacons content with the traditional view of seeking ordination in response to a deeply perceived prompting from God? To what extent were women deacons conscious of seeking ordination as a way of giving greater authority to their ministry? To what extent did women deacons seek ordination as a deliberate strategy to change the perceived sexist nature of the church?

The second issue concerns the difficulties which women deacons perceived as standing in their path to ordination. To what extent were women deacons conscious of their gender making things more difficult for them? To what extent had they felt inwardly discouraged from seeking ordination? Or to what extent had they experienced outward discouragement from others?

Overview

Traditionally the move to seek ordination within the Church of England has been expressed in terms of a direct call from God. It is the notion that ordination is a response to a prompting from God. The women deacons were no exception to this traditional view of ordination. The personal belief that God wished them to be ordained is overwhelmingly the strongest reason for seeking ordination among the women deacons (97%).

Table 1 Call to ministry

	Yes %	? %	No %
I sought ordination because I believed God wished me to be ordained	97	3	1
I sought ordination because it gave greater authority to my ministry	53	14	33
I sought ordination to help change the sexist nature of the church	17	11	72
My gender made it more difficult for me to seek ordination	46	12	43
I often felt inwardly discouraged from seeking ordination	22	10	68
Others often discouraged me from seeking ordination	12	6	82

At the same time, over half (53%) of the women deacons were conscious of seeking ordination in order to give greater authority to their ministry. Less than one third (33%) rejected this as a reason for ordination. This could imply a difference in theological perspective between those who see authority in ministry coming directly from the divine call and those who see authority in ministry coming from the public recognition of that divine call conferred through ordination.

Less than one fifth (17%) of the women deacons sought ordination as a strategy to change the perceived sexist nature of the church. The majority of the women deacons (72%) deliberately rejected the view that they had sought ordination in order to change the sexist nature of the church, leaving the remaining 11% who were not certain whether this specific aim had played a part in their motivation to seek ordination.

The path to ordination was not necessarily a smooth one for many of the women deacons. The survey results show that nearly half (46%) of the women deacons found that their gender made it more difficult for them to seek ordination. However, almost an equal number (43%) did not find that their gender made a difference, leaving 12% who were not certain whether or not their gender had made their path to ordination more difficult.

Over two thirds (68%) of the women deacons had not felt inwardly discouraged from seeking ordination. This would suggest a strong inward conviction. However, the women deacons were more likely to have experienced feelings of inward discouragement than to have felt discouraged by others. Thus, 22% had felt inwardly discouraged, as compared with 12% who had felt discouraged from seeking ordination by others. This issue, however, shows that a significant number of women deacons (one in every eight) had experienced others actively discouraging them from the course to which they believed God had called them. On the other hand over four fifths (82%) of the women deacons had not felt discouraged by others from seeking ordination.

Does age make a difference?

The clear sense that the fundamental motivation toward ordination lay in the divine call remained constant among the four cohorts of women deacons (those under the age of forty, those in their forties, those in their fifties and those aged sixty or over). The proportion who said that they sought ordination because they believed God wished them to be ordained varied by no more than just two percentage points from 96% among those under the age of forty to 98% among those in their forties.

In other ways, however, clear differences emerge between the four cohorts concerning certain aspects of their motivation toward ordination. The question of the authority given by ordination was of greater importance to the older women deacons. While 43% of those under the age of forty considered that they sought ordination because it gave greater authority to their ministry, the proportion rose to 50% among those in their forties, 58% among those in their fifties and 62% among those aged sixty or over.

On the other hand, the question of seeing the ordination of women as helping to change the sexist nature of the church was of greater importance to the younger women deacons. Thus, one in four of the women deacons under the age of 40 (25%) said that she sought ordination to help change the sexist nature of the church, compared with 15% of those in their forties, 17% of those in their fifties and 14% of those aged sixty or over.

The proportion of women deacons who felt that their gender had made it more difficult for them to seek ordination remained roughly consistent throughout the four age cohorts, varying by no more than three percentage points from 48% among the women deacons under the age of forty to 45% among those in their forties, 45% among those in their fifties and 46% among those aged sixty or over.

The statistics show that the sense of being discouraged from seeking ordination is somewhat lower among the youngest cohort of women deacons. Here the contrast is clear between the women deacons under the age of forty and those in their fifties. Thus, 18% of the women deacons under the age of forty said that they often felt inwardly discouraged from seeking ordination, compared with 25% of those in their fifties. A similar, but less significant, trend is found in relation to external discouragement, with 11% of those under the age of forty saying that others often discouraged them from seeking ordination, compared with 14% of those in their fifties.

Does marital status make a difference?

Marital status makes only marginal differences to the proportion of women deacons who were certain that the fundamental motivation toward ordination lay in the divine call. The statistics show that this certainly was the case for 98% of the widowed, 97% of the married, 96% of the single and 95% of the divorced women deacons.

The question of the authority given by ordination was of greatest importance to the widowed and divorced women deacons and of least importance to the single women deacons. While 46% of the single women deacons considered that they sought ordination because it gave greater authority to their ministry, the proportion rose to 55% among the married, 62% among the divorced and 64% among the widowed.

The question of seeing the ordination of women as helping to change the sexist nature of the church was of greatest importance to the divorced women deacons and of the least importance to the single women deacons. Only 11% of the single women deacons said that they sought ordination to help change the sexist nature of the church, compared with 25% of the divorced women deacons. This view was also adopted by 19% of the widowed and 21% of the married women deacons.

The single women deacons were somewhat less likely to feel that their gender had make it more difficult for them to seek ordination. This view was taken by 41% of the single women deacons, compared with 48% of the married, 48% of the divorced and 49% of the widowed.

The single women deacons were also less likely to have felt internal or external discouragement from seeking ordination. As far as internal discouragement is concerned, the strongest contrast is between the single and the married women deacons.

In this sense 26% of the married women deacons said that they often felt inwardly discouraged from seeking ordination, compared with 16% of the single women deacons. This view was also taken by 19% of the widowed and 23% of the divorced women deacons. A major source of internal discouragement may, therefore, seem to centre on the perceived potential conflict between ordained ministry and demands of family life.

As far as external discouragement is concerned, the strongest contrast is between the single and the divorced women deacons. In this sense, 18% of the divorced women deacons said that others often discouraged them from seeking ordination, compared with 10% of the single women deacons. This view was also taken by 12% of the married and 17% of the widowed women deacons. These findings suggest that there may be some link between the call to ministry and marital breakdown among the divorced women deacons.

Overall, the statistics show that the smoothest path to ordination was experienced by the single women deacons and that the single women deacons were the least likely to have sought ordination as a source of authority for their ministry.

Does church tradition make a difference?

Women deacons across the church traditions are clearly united in the view that their ordination to the diaconate was in direct response to a call from God. Thus, 98% of those who identified with the Evangelical wing, 97% of those who identified with the Catholic wing and 96% of those who identified with the middle way of Anglicanism agreed that they sought ordination because they believed God wished them to be ordained.

The question of the authority given by ordination was seen to be most important by the women deacons who identified with the middle way of Anglicanism (55%), compared with 52% of Catholics and 51% of Evangelicals.

The question of seeing the ordination of women as helping to change the sexist nature of the church was of much less importance to those on the Evangelical wing of the church. While one in every five women deacons identifying with the Catholic wing (20%) or middle way of Anglicanism (21%) agreed that she sought ordination to help change the sexist nature of the church, the proportion fell to one in every ten women deacons identifying with the Evangelical wing (9%).

It was the Catholic wing of the Anglican church which had the greatest difficulty in accepting the ordination of women. It might be anticipated, therefore, that the women deacons identifying with the Catholic wing should have experienced the least smooth journey to ordination. The statistics clearly support this view.

Nearly three in every five women deacons (57%) who identified with the Catholic wing of the church said that their gender made it more difficult for them to seek ordination, compared with two in every five (39%) who identified with the Evangelical wing of the church and 45% who identified with the middle way of Anglicanism.

Similarly, one in four of the Catholic women deacons (26%) said that she often felt inwardly discouraged from seeking ordination, compared with 20% of the Evangelical and 22% of the middle way women deacons. One in five of the Catholic women deacons (20%) said that others often discouraged her from seeking ordination, compared with 10% of the Evangelical and 10% of the middle way women deacons.

Overall, these statistics show that women within the Catholic wing of the church experienced a tougher path to ordination.

Are non-stipendiaries different?

For some the transition to non-stipendiary ministry may seem less radical and less disruptive than the transition to stipendiary ministry. After all, many non-stipendiary ministers remain in their same secular employment, remain living in the same house and may even remain serving in a church which they have known for some years. Many non-stipendiary ministers do not experience the disruption of going away for residential full-time training. Of even greater significance is the practical debate regarding the role of the local congregation in calling candidates for non-stipendiary ministry, especially for what is becoming known as local non-stipendiary ministry. In spite of these differences the women deacons serving in non-stipendiary ministry are no less likely than women deacons serving in stipendiary ministry to be certain that their ordination came about in a direct response to God's call. Thus, 97% of the stipendiary and 96% of the non-stipendiary women deacons said that they sought ordination because they believed God wished them to be ordained.

The views of ordination held by stipendiary and non-stipendiary women deacons differed in some important ways. Women deacons in stipendiary ministry were less concerned with the authority conferred by ordination than women deacons serving in non-stipendiary ministry. Thus, 61% of non-stipendiary women deacons said that they sought ordination because it gave greater authority to their ministry, compared with 47% of stipendiary women deacons.

On the other hand, there is comparatively little difference between the views of stipendiary and non-stipendiary women deacons on the question of seeing the ordination of women as changing the sexist nature of the church. Thus, 13% of the non-stipendiary and 16% of the stipendiary women deacons said that they sought ordination to help change the sexist nature of the church.

Gender is perceived to be no less an obstacle for non-stipendiary ministry than for stipendiary ministry. It was the view of 43% of the non-stipendiary and 45% of the stipendiary women deacons that their gender made it more difficult for them to seek ordination.

It is the non-stipendiary women deacons who experienced the greater discouragement on the path to ordination, both internally and externally. Three out of every ten non-stipendiary women deacons (30%) said that they often felt inward discouragement from seeking ordination, compared with two out of every ten stipendiary women deacons (20%). Similarly, 13% of the non-stipendiary women deacons said that others often discouraged them from seeking ordination, compared with 10% of the stipendiary women deacons.

Overall, these statistics suggest that the path to ordination may have been somewhat tougher for those wishing to serve in non-stipendiary ministry.

Hearing the stories

Listening to the women deacons reflect on their personal call to ministry four main issues come through.

First, the women deacons expressed a strong sense of a call from God. This was expressed as both a sudden and quite dramatic realisation, as one woman wrote.

> There was an experience during a communion service, when I experienced a sense of standing in the priest's place and it seemed natural and right. *(non-stipendiary, assistant curate aged 41)*

Equally it was expressed as a gradual but growing awareness as this woman deacon explained.

> My decision to enter ordained ministry was very gradual in that I was aware for twenty years. *(stipendiary, assistant curate aged 45)*

Second, listening to the women deacons' stories, it is clear that a number of them had to hold firmly to their call to ministry through many years of being prevented from fulfilling their vocation because of their gender.

> I had a fleeting sense of vocation at thirteen but was the wrong gender. *(stipendiary, parish deacon aged 48)*

Another woman summed this issue up simply.

> I believe that, had I been a man, I would have sought ordination in 1958. However, the door was firmly shut - obviously so for many years. *(stipendiary, deacon in charge aged 58)*

Third, the women deacons remained sure of their vocation despite being discouraged by others. For example, one woman deacon recorded that her path was blocked by simple misinformation.

> When I felt God calling me to ordination in 1978 I was told by my then incumbent that married women could not be deaconesses. When I discovered I was maritally able to be ordained I went forward for selection. *(non-stipendiary, parish deacon aged 60)*

Listening to the stories of other women deacons it is clear that the official stance of the church on women in ministry made the path to fulfilling their call to ministry, at times, almost impossible.

> When I was young I dismissed from my mind thoughts of being ordained. The church made it impossible for women. *(non-stipendiary, assistant curate, aged 67)*

It is not surprising that this situation caused problems for many women as they tried to respond to their sense of vocation. One woman deacon summed it up as follows.

> I have found my vocation a particularly messy affair. *(stipendiary, cathedral clergy aged 36)*

Fourth, it is clear that, despite the difficulties the women deacons have faced over the years as change has slowly come to the church, many have found their call to ministry has begun to be fulfilled.

> I have known since I was seventeen years old of my vocation to priesthood, so I have gone through each door as it has opened...and now at long last priesthood. *(non-stipendiary, parish deacon aged 70)*

These accounts raise important issues for the church. This group of women have been unable to follow the path to ministry traditionally open to men and have been prevented from testing their vocation by the church. The church can learn a great deal from listening to how these women have dealt with the rejection of their call, often over many years, and the way their ministry has developed in view of this. One woman summed up her response like this.

> I am pleased to have taken heed of God's call and humbled to be privileged to be called. It is worth the struggle. *(non-stipendiary, assistant curate aged 47)*

2 Selection

Introduction

The gateway to ordination within the Anglican church is securely guarded by a rigorous selection process. Candidates for ministry are invited to have their vocation properly tested by a board of selectors. The women in the present study are those who survived the selection process. To what extent were they able to look back on the selection process as a positive experience, or to what extent did they feel that their experience was a negative one?

The selectors themselves are people who have been trained to give the candidates a fair hearing, but also to test their vocation and their suitability for training in depth and with thoroughness. What did these women make of the selectors themselves? Did they feel that the selectors treated them fairly and in a friendly manner? Did any of them feel that the selectors failed to take them seriously, or treated them in a hostile or patronising way? Did any of them feel disadvantaged in the selection process by their gender?

Overview

The survey results make it clear that, while three quarters (77%) of the women deacons were left with a positive experience of the selection process, another one in every four was left with a less positive view of the process. Even for those who were recommended for training, the selection process could be a gruelling and exhausting experience.

Although as many as one in four of the women deacons found the selection process less than a positive experience, the level of criticism raised against the selectors themselves is very small. Out of every hundred of the women deacons, two felt that the selectors failed to take them seriously, four felt that the selectors treated them in an unfriendly or hostile manner, five felt that the selectors viewed their gender negatively and

Table 2 Selection

	Yes %	? %	No %
The selection process was a positive experience for me	77	9	14
The selectors:			
treated me in a friendly manner	91	6	4
treated me fairly	88	7	6
treated me in a hostile manner	4	4	92
did not take me seriously	2	5	92
viewed my gender negatively	5	11	84
treated me in a patronising manner	10	7	83

six felt that the selectors treated them unfairly. The proportion rose to ten in every hundred, however, who felt that the selectors had treated them in a patronising manner.

When the 'not certain' responses are also taken into account, the level of criticism raised against the selectors may appear just a little higher. On this account, out of every hundred women deacons, seven were not convinced that the selectors had taken them seriously, eight were not convinced that hostility had not been shown to them, ten were not convinced that they had been treated in a friendly manner, thirteen were not convinced that they had been treated fairly, sixteen were not convinced that their gender had not been viewed negatively and seventeen were not convinced that they had not been treated in a patronising manner.

These statistics suggest that, overall, the selectors were making a good job of the responsibility entrusted to them by the church, at least from the perspective of those who were selected for training. At the same time, however, two warning signals are issued by the statistics. First, the fact that one in ten of the successful candidates felt patronised by the selectors suggests that selector training should give more attention to this aspect of interpersonal relationships. Second, the fact that one in six of the successful candidates remained uncertain that their gender had not been viewed negatively by the selectors suggests that greater attention should have been given to offering appropriate affirmation to the women candidates.

Does age make a difference?

The statistics make it clear that the older women deacons held a more positive view of the selection process than those under the age of forty. While 77% of the women deacons in their forties, 81% of those in their fifties and 78% of those aged sixty or over reported that the selection process was a positive experience for them, the proportion fell to 68% of the women deacons under the age of forty.

The most serious complaint of the women deacons in the youngest cohort was that the selectors treated them in a patronising manner. While only 4% of the women deacons aged sixty or over felt that the selectors treated then in a patronising manner, the proportions rose steadily to 8% among those in their fifties, 11% among those in their forties and 15% among those under forty years of age.

A similar trend is revealed concerning how the candidates perceived the selectors' attitude toward their gender. While only 3% of the women deacons aged sixty or over felt that the selectors viewed their gender negatively, the proportion rose slightly to 4% among those in their fifties, 5% among those in their forties and 7% among those under forty years of age.

The trend is found again in assessing traces of hostility in the selectors' attitude toward the candidate. While only 1% of the women deacons aged sixty or over felt that the selectors treated them in a hostile manner, the proportion rose slightly to 3% among those in their fifties, 5% among those in their forties, and 6% among those under forty years of age.

Overall, the women deacons in the youngest cohort were the least likely to have felt that the selectors had treated them fairly. Thus, 18% of the women deacons under the age of forty were not at all sure that the selectors had treated them fairly, compared with 12% of those in their forties, and 9% of those in their fifties and those aged sixty or over.

Does marital status make a difference?

The group of women deacons with the least positive attitude toward the selection process are those who have experienced divorce. While on average 77% of the women deacons found that the selection process was a positive experience for them, the proportion fell to 72% among the divorced.

In particular the divorced women deacons were more inclined to feel that the selectors treated them in a patronising manner and viewed their gender negatively. While on average 10% of the women deacons felt that the selectors treated them in a patronising manner, the proportion rose to 15% among the divorced. While on average 5% of the women deacons felt that the selectors viewed their gender negatively, the proportion rose to 10% among the divorced.

Generally the married and the single women deacons held similar attitudes toward the selection process. For example, 75% of the single women deacons found that the selection process was a positive experience for them, and so did 77% of the married women deacons. Similarly, 87% of the single women deacons felt that the selectors treated them fairly, and so did 88% of the married women deacons. Looked at from another perspective, 2% of the single women deacons felt that the selectors did not take them seriously, and so did 3% of the married women deacons. Similarly, 10% of the single women deacons felt that the selectors treated them in a patronising manner, and so did 10% of the married women deacons.

One way of looking at these statistics is to suggest that the women deacons who have experienced difficulties in their marriage relationship are also more likely to have experienced relational difficulties with selectors.

Does church tradition make a difference?

The previous chapter has made it clear that women deacons within the Catholic tradition found the call to ordination more difficult than women deacons within the Evangelical tradition. The statistics in the present section, however, demonstrate that this greater sense of difficulty did not follow the women deacons from the Catholic tradition into the selection process. Catholics and Evangelicals perceived the selection process in very similar ways.

While 79% of the Evangelical women deacons reported that the selection process was a positive experience for them, so did 77% of the Catholic women deacons. While 91% of the Evangelical women deacons felt that the selectors treated them in a friendly manner, so did 89% of the Catholic women deacons.

Looked at from the opposite perspective, while 2% of the Evangelical women deacons felt that the selectors did not take them seriously, 4% of the Catholic women deacons felt the same way. While 9% of the Evangelical women deacons felt that the selectors treated them in a patronising manner, 11% of the Catholic women deacons felt the same way.

On just two issues in this part of the survey the Catholic women deacons gave a significantly less positive response than the Evangelical women deacons. The Catholic women deacons were less likely than the Evangelical women deacons to feel that the selectors treated them fairly (86% compared with 90%). The Catholic women deacons were more likely than the Evangelical women deacons to feel that the selectors viewed their gender negatively (9% compared with 4%).

The response toward the selection process of the women deacons who identified with the middle way of Anglicanism did not differ from the overall response of all the women deacons considered together.

Overall, church tradition does not seem to be all that strongly related to how the women deacons perceived the selection process. The selection process, therefore, seems to have treated women from different church traditions in comparable ways.

Are non-stipendiaries different?

The previous chapter has suggested that the path to ordination may have been somewhat tougher for those women who wished to serve in non-stipendiary ministry. The statistics in the present section, however, suggest that those who were heading for stipendiary ministry and those who were heading for non-stipendiary ministry had a very similar experience of the selection process. On the majority of the issues raised in this section the two groups varied by no more than two percentage points.

Beginning with a positive perspective, 87% of the non-stipendiary women deacons and 89% of the stipendiary women deacons felt that the selectors treated them fairly. Taking a less positive perspective, 5% of the non-stipendiary women deacons and 3% of the stipendiary women deacons felt that the selectors treated them in a hostile manner. Exactly the same proportions of non-stipendiary and stipendiary women deacons felt that the selectors did not take them seriously (3%). Exactly the same proportion of non-stipendiary and stipendiary women deacons felt that the selectors viewed their gender negatively (4%).

On just two issues in this section did the views of non-stipendiary and stipendiary women deacons vary by more than two percentage points. On the one hand, the non-stipendiary women deacons were marginally more likely than the stipendiary women deacons to have considered overall that the selection process was a positive experience for them (79% compared with 76%). On the other hand, the non-stipendiary women deacons were marginally less likely than the stipendiary women deacons to have considered that the selectors treated them in a friendly manner (88% compared with 92%).

Overall, therefore, the selection process seems to have been perceived as treating candidates for non-stipendiary ministry and candidates for stipendiary ministry in very similar ways.

Hearing the stories

Listening to the experiences of the women deacons with regard to the selection process three main problems are clear.

First, for a number of women it took more than one selection conference before they were accepted for ministry. One woman deacon put it as follows.

> I had to battle through four selection conferences. *(non-stipendiary, assistant curate aged 57)*

It is clear from this that those who are not successful in their first selection conference(s) need support after what is often perceived as a rejection of their vocation. One woman deacon said that her:

> first (selection conference) eighteen months before was a dreadful experience and took a long time to get over. *(stipendiary, parish deacon aged 38)*

Second, there are those who felt that they had been successful in the selection process only because they had applied for a particular type of ministry. This woman deacon's story clearly demonstrated the point.

> I was told, not asked, that as a married woman only non-stipendiary ministry would be open to me. *(stipendiary, parish deacon aged 56)*

Third, for a number of the women the attitude of some of the selectors caused difficulties. For instance this woman deacon experienced open hostility when:

> one selector was hostile and unfair. *(stipendiary, parish deacon aged 59)*

It is clear, however, that selectors cannot be viewed as a homogeneous group, as the following woman deacon described from her experience.

Some were intelligent, well trained, interested people, polite and kind. Some were rude and inconsiderate. *(non-stipendiary, part-time assistant curate and part-time secular employment aged 47)*

Accounts like these do raise questions with regard to the selection and training of the selectors. It would seem that, although the majority of the selectors are doing their jobs well, there are others who clearly are not.

3 First appointment

Introduction

For many clergy, both male and female, their first appointment can be of fundamental importance in shaping their future attitude toward ministry and in developing their practical skills in ministry. Much may depend, therefore, on the ways in which training incumbents feel willing or able to share the responsibilities of ministry with their new and junior colleagues. This is an issue of as much concern to the newly ordained clergywomen as to the newly ordained clergymen.

This chapter sets out to explore, therefore, the extent to which the women deacons felt that their training incumbent was really willing to share ministry with them. How many of the women deacons felt that their training incumbent gave them an *equal* share of the responsibility in parish ministry? Or how many felt properly included in making parish decisions? How many women deacons felt that their training incumbent failed to delegate sufficient aspects of ministry to them? Or how many felt exploited by having too much work delegated to them? To what extent did the women deacons feel that sufficient use was made of their talents by their training incumbent? Or to what extent did they feel that they had been properly supported by adequate feedback?

Overview

The survey results demonstrate that only about one third of the women deacons felt that they had been given an equal share of the responsibility by their training incumbent (36%), while half were quite clear that this was not the case (50%). The positive interpretation of these figures is that training incumbents may be showing proper respect for the inexperience of their junior colleagues. The less positive interpretation of these figures is that the junior clergy will not be adequately trained to accept responsibility unless they can experience the risks as well as the joys of such responsibility during the period of their training curacy.

Table 3 First appointment

	Yes %	? %	No %
My first incumbent:			
did not delegate enough tasks to me	32	8	60
delegated too many tasks to me	11	9	80
did not make sufficient use of my talents	32	9	58
did not give me sufficient feedback	40	7	53
included me in making parish decisions	62	11	28
gave me an equal share of the responsibility	36	14	50

On the other hand, twice as many women deacons felt that they had been properly included in making parish decisions (62%) as felt that they had been excluded from making parish decisions (28%).

Overall quite a high proportion of women deacons (32%) felt that their training incumbent had failed to delegate enough tasks to them during their first years in ministry, while only 11% complained that too many tasks had been delegated to them during this time.

As many as two in every five of the women deacons (40%) felt that they had not been given sufficient feedback by their training incumbent. As many as one in every three of the women deacons (32%) felt that her training incumbent had not made sufficient use of her talents.

The composite picture to emerge from these statistics does not present a healthy picture of the training which supposedly took place during the first curacy of these women deacons. Four out of every ten women deacons felt deprived of adequate feedback on their developing ministry. Three out of every ten women deacons felt under deployed during this stage of ministry. Three out of every ten women deacons felt that their own talents had not been properly used. Three out of every ten women deacons felt that they had enjoyed no real part in shaping parish policy.

Statistics such as these raise serious questions regarding the extent to which training incumbents had been properly prepared for the important and skilled task of training women deacons during their formative years of ministry.

Does age make a difference?

In many ways similar experiences of their first appointment were reported by all four cohorts of women deacons. For example, around one in three of the women deacons under the age of forty complained that her first incumbent did not delegate enough tasks to her (30%), and so did 33% of those in their forties, 32% of those in their fifties and 33% of those aged sixty or over. Similarly, around one in ten of the women deacons under the age of forty complained that her first incumbent delegated too many tasks to her (9%), and so did 13% of the women deacons in their forties, 10% of the women deacons in their fifties and 11% of the women deacons aged sixty or over.

Where differences do emerge between the four cohorts of women deacons, these differences emerge most clearly in contrasting the cohort aged under forty with the cohort aged sixty or over. On the one hand, the older cohort felt more trusted and more responsible. Thus, 41% of the women deacons aged sixty or over felt that their first incumbent gave them an equal share of the responsibility, compared with 36% of the women deacons aged under forty.

On the other hand, the older cohort felt less valued for who they were. Thus, 35% of the women deacons aged sixty or over felt that their first incumbent did not make sufficient use of their talents, compared with 30% of the women deacons aged under forty.

The other main difference between the youngest cohort and the oldest cohort concerns their attitude toward the feedback given by their training incumbent. While four in every ten women deacons under the age of forty considered that their training incumbent failed to give them sufficient feedback (41%), this was the case for three in every ten women deacons aged sixty or over (31%). It may well be the case that the older women deacons both expected and needed less feedback.

Does marital status make a difference?

The experiences of the single and the married women deacons of their first appointment were very similar. For example, 30% of the single women deacons complained that their first incumbent did not delegate enough tasks to them, and so did 31% of the married women deacons. Similarly, 10% of the single women deacons complained that their first incumbent delegated too many tasks to them, and so did 11% of the married women deacons.

While 30% of the single women deacons felt that their first incumbent did not make sufficient use of their talents, so did 32% of the married women deacons. While 40% of the single women deacons felt that their first incumbent did not give them sufficient feedback, so did 39% of the married women deacons.

While 63% of the single women deacons felt that their first incumbent included them in making parish decisions, so did 63% of the married women deacons. While 36% of the single women deacons felt that their first incumbent gave them an equal share of the responsibility, so did 37% of the married women deacons.

It is the divorced women deacons, however, who stand apart as having a somewhat different attitude toward their first appointment. Overall, the divorced women deacons displayed a less positive attitude toward their first appointment. This point can be illustrated by contrasting the perceptions of the divorced women deacons with the perceptions of the married women deacons.

While 31% of the married women deacons felt that their first incumbent did not delegate enough tasks to them, the proportion rose to 43% among the divorced women deacons. At the same time, while 11% of the married women deacons felt that their first incumbent delegated too many tasks to them, the proportion rose to 18% among the divorced women deacons.

While 32% of the married women deacons felt that their first incumbent did not make sufficient use of their talents, the proportion rose to 43% of the divorced women deacons. While 63% of the married women deacons felt that their first incumbent included them in making parish decisions, the proportion fell to 52% among the divorced women deacons.

These statistics suggest that training incumbents may need to be particularly sensitive to the needs and expectations of curates who have experienced divorce.

Does the church tradition make a difference?

Chapter one drew attention to the fact that women deacons from the Catholic wing of the church found more obstacles on the path to ordination than women deacons from the Evangelical wing of the church. The statistics in the present chapter, however, suggest that, once ordained, women deacons from the Catholic wing and from the Evangelical wing of the church share similar perceptions of their first appointment.

For example, 32% of the Evangelical women deacons complained that their first incumbent did not delegate enough tasks to them, and so did 34% of the Catholic women deacons. Similarly, 11% of the Evangelical women deacons complained that their first incumbent delegated too many tasks to them, and so did 13% of the Catholic women deacons.

While 64% of the Evangelical women deacons felt that their first incumbent included them in making parish decisions, so did 62% of the Catholic women deacons. While 39% of the Evangelical women deacons complained that their first incumbent did not give them sufficient feedback, so did 41% of the Catholic women deacons.

The perceptions of the Catholic and Evangelical women deacons only differed significantly in respect of two of the four issues included in this section. On both of these two issues, however, the Catholic women deacons reported less satisfactory experiences. While 30% of the Evangelical women deacons complained that their first incumbent did not make sufficient use of their talents, the proportion rose to 36% among the Catholic women deacons. While 38% of the Evangelical women deacons felt that their first incumbent gave them an equal share of the responsibility, the proportion fell slightly to 34% among the Catholic women deacons.

The response of the women deacons who identify with the middle way of Anglicanism toward their first appointment did not differ from the overall response of all the women deacons considered together.

Are non-stipendiaries different?

While the stipendiary minister is holding her first appointment as a full-time training curacy, the non-stipendiary minister usually has much less time to devote to the parish and much less opportunity to benefit from the training which the parish can offer.

On the one hand, because they were often only part-time in parish ministry, some non-stipendiary women deacons complained that their training incumbent expected too much of them and made demands as if they were in the parish full-time. On the other hand, some non-stipendiary women deacons had the very opposite experience and complained that, because they are only in parish ministry part-time, their training incumbent tended to overlook their proper contribution to parish life. Other non-stipendiary ministers, who were not in simultaneous secular employment, may have chosen to serve full-time in their training curacy.

The statistics show that, overall, the non-stipendiary women deacons were less inclined than the stipendiary women deacons to feel that they were overworked in their first appointment. For example, while 12% of the stipendiary women deacons felt that their first incumbent delegated too many tasks to them, the proportion fell to 7% among the non-stipendiary women deacons. On the other hand, while 31% of the stipendiary women deacons felt that their first incumbent did not delegate enough tasks to them, the proportion rose to 36% among the non-stipendiary women deacons.

As part-time members of the parish staff the non-stipendiary women deacons were less likely than stipendiary women deacons to feel that they had a full part to play in parish life. For example, while 63% of the stipendiary women deacons felt that their first incumbent included them in making parish decisions, the proportion fell to 59% among the non-stipendiary women deacons. On the other hand, while 38% of the stipendiary women deacons felt that their first incumbent gave them an equal share of responsibility, the proportion fell to 31% among the non-stipendiary women deacons.

Overall, these findings suggest that training programmes for training incumbents may need to give particular attention to the issues surrounding the proper provision for non-stipendiary curates.

Hearing the stories

The women deacons' reflections on their first appointment highlight four important issues for the church structure. First, women deacons going into ministry more often than not failed to fit the usual patterns of male curates. The church had yet to adjust to this fact as was recognised in two different ways by two women deacons. For one of the women the experience was more negative than for the other.

> My first incumbent in many ways was supportive yet found me being a woman in ministry difficult not because we didn't get on personally but because of his own expectations of what a curate was to be regardless of gender. *(stipendiary, cathedral clergy aged 36)*

> My experience has generally been positive. Being young and single I fitted easily into the usual pattern of male curates. *(stipendiary, parish deacon aged 32)*

Second, the church was not used to working with clergy couples. There was no clear system in place for dealing with this issue, as is illustrated by this woman deacon.

> When I was first licensed, I was married to a serving priest. We were in the same parish. There was little experience of working with clergy couples and I had no real role of my own. There followed many frustrating years of being just an NSM attached to my husband. *(stipendiary, sector minister aged 37)*

The problems of serving the first curacy as a non-stipendiary minister in the same parish as her spouse were compounded for some women deacons when a change of jobs was offered to the husband. Do they move on together, move on separately to different parishes, or can the woman deacon be left serving in her old parish? It is clear from the following account that for this woman deacon ministry ceased to be possible once her husband moved job, due to a lack of understanding particularly on the part of the bishop.

> I became my husband's NSM, but when he moved out of parochial ministry into sector ministry I was without a church. I now have to earn money to pay our mortgage and have been told by the bishop I have to become an NSM before he thinks about stipendiary ministry. *(secular employment aged 49)*

It is clear that for both of these women deacons their first appointment proved to be unsatisfactory because the church could not deal effectively with placing clergy couples.

Third, a change of incumbent during a first appointment is potentially unsettling for the curate. Although it is not always possible for the same incumbent to see a first curacy through from beginning to end, if the assistant curate is not properly consulted and involved in the change there can be problems. This point is made starkly by the following woman deacon who contrasts her experiences under two training incumbents within the same parish.

> The first was very encouraging, the second very discouraging. *(stipendiary, parish deacon aged 56)*

Fourth, it would seem that most women deacons experienced a positive sharing of ministry with their training incumbent.

> He (my incumbent) basically said look to see what needs doing, and get on with it. So his help in one way was very little but I relished being able to get on with it and we got on really well together. *(stipendiary, deacon in charge aged 53)*

This experience of being given a 'free hand' as a positive experience was emphasised by other deacons, while at the same time acknowledging the lack of constructive help which this approach so often implies.

> Although I have said the first incumbent gave little help in developing certain aspects of ministry he helped by allowing me to have a free hand in all my public worshipping and local community. *(non-stipendiary, assistant curate, aged 53)*

4 Training incumbent

Introduction

As long as the clerical profession remained an all-male domain, the relationship between training incumbent and curate was uncomplicated by gender differences. As long as the Church of England accepted women in the order of deacon, but not in the order of priest, newly ordained women deacons invariably found themselves assigned to a male priest as training incumbent. Many of these male priests may have been inadequately prepared for the inevitable change in relational dynamics when they received their first woman deacon as curate.

This chapter sets out to explore, therefore, the extent to which the women deacons perceived their relationship with their training incumbent to have been adversely influenced by the difference in gender. How many of the women deacons felt that their training incumbent was uncomfortable working with a female colleague? Or how many felt that their training incumbent was generally unhelpful and unconstructive toward them? To what extent did the women deacons perceive their training incumbent to have been overprotective of them?

The close working relationship between training incumbent and curate may also introduce new suspicions and strains on existing personal relationships. How many women deacons felt that their presence in the parish was experienced as a threat by their training incumbent's wife? Or how many felt that their own partner experienced the training incumbent as a threat?

Overview

The survey results show that the majority of women deacons experienced their training incumbent as helpful and constructive (69%). This still left three in every ten women deacons who were not confident of such support (31%), or two in every ten who experienced their training incumbent as unhelpful and unconstructive (19%).

As many as two in every ten women deacons (20%) recognised that their training incumbent felt uncomfortable working with a female colleague, while a further one in every ten (11%) was suspicious that this might have been the case.

Table 4 Training incumbent

	Yes %	? %	No %
My training incumbent:			
was generally helpful and constructive	69	12	19
felt uncomfortable working with a female colleague	20	11	69
felt threatened by me	32	14	54
was too protective of me	11	8	81
My training incumbent's wife felt threatened by me	20	18	62
My partner felt threatened by my training incumbent	6	7	87

Some of the women ordained to the diaconate between 1987 and 1994 were mature and competent individuals who had maintained successful careers prior to ordination. One in every three of these women (32%) recognised that her training incumbent felt threatened by her. At the same time, one in every ten (11%) felt that her training incumbent treated her in an overprotective manner.

The impact of a woman deacon in the parish on the training incumbent's wife was a matter of concern to a large number of women. One in every five women deacons was convinced that her training incumbent's wife had felt threatened by her (20%), while a further one in every five remained anxious that this might have been the case (18%). These statistics suggest that many training incumbents had not been properly prepared for the abrupt transition from training male curates to training female curates and had not sufficiently anticipated and addressed the impact that this transition may have had on their own family life.

At the same time, about one in every eight women deacons (13%) showed some anxiety regarding the impact exerted by her training incumbent over her own partner.

Does age make a difference?

The experiences of the four cohorts of women deacons (those under the age of forty, those in their forties, those in their fifties and those aged sixty or over) regarding their training incumbents were all very similar. Nevertheless, some contrasts emerged between the cohorts which deserve comment.

The age cohort with the most positive attitude toward their training incumbent was the women deacons aged sixty or over. The age cohort with the least positive attitude toward their training incumbent was the women deacons in their forties. The following statistics illustrate the contrast between these two age groups.

While three quarters (74%) of the women deacons aged sixty or over found their training incumbent generally helpful and constructive, the proportion fell to two thirds (66%) of the women deacons in their forties. While one in four (26%) of the women deacons aged sixty or over considered that her training incumbent felt threatened by her, the proportion rose to more than one in three (36%) of the women deacons in their forties. While 18% of the women deacons aged sixty or over had concluded that their training incumbent felt uncomfortable working with a female colleague, the proportion rose to 22% of the women deacons in their forties.

Although the contrast is clearly less strong, women deacons in their forties reported a slightly less positive attitude toward their training incumbent than their colleagues under the age of forty and their colleagues in their fifties. These statistics suggest that the cohort of women deacons in their forties might have presented particular challenges to their training incumbent. At the same time, this cohort might have benefited from more sensitive placing than was in fact realised by the church.

Does marital status make a difference?

The attitudes of the married and single women deacons toward their training incumbent were really quite similar. For example, 69% of the married women deacons and 70% of the single women deacons found their training incumbent generally helpful and constructive. Similarly, 30% of the married women deacons and 32% of the single women deacons thought that their training incumbent had felt threatened by them.

On the other hand, the married women deacons were slightly more likely than the single women deacons to have sensed that their training incumbent felt uncomfortable working with a female colleague (20% compared with 16%) or that their training incumbent was too protective of them (13% compared with 9%).

The real issue focused by an analysis of marital status, however, concerns the distinctive experience of the divorced women deacons. This group reported a much less positive attitude toward their training incumbents than either their married or single colleagues. For example, while 70% of the single women deacons found their training incumbent generally helpful and constructive, the proportion fell to 63% of the divorced women deacons. While 32% of the single women deacons reported that their training incumbent felt threatened by them, the proportion rose to 37% of the divorced women deacons. While 16% of the single women deacons found that their training incumbent felt uncomfortable working with a female colleague, the proportion more than doubled among the divorced women deacons to 37%. These statistics suggest that the church may have been wiser to have given greater consideration to the issues raised by divorce for the relationship between training incumbent and female curate.

In some ways the experience of widowed women deacons is similar to the experience of married women deacons. For example, 69% of the married and 70% of the widowed women deacons found their training incumbent generally helpful and constructive. In other ways, however, the experience of widowed women deacons is closer to the experience of divorced women deacons. For example, 39% of the widowed and 37% of the divorced women deacons considered that their training incumbent felt threatened by them, compared with 30% of the married women deacons.

The marital status of the women deacons also has significant implications for their perceptions of the impact on their training incumbent's wife and on their own partner. The divorced women deacons were much more likely to consider that their training incumbent's wife felt threatened by them (33% compared with 20% of the single, 19% of the married and 20% of the widowed). They were also much more likely to consider that their own partners felt threatened by their training incumbent (22% compared with 13% of the single, 5% of the married and 7% of the widowed).

Does church tradition make a difference?

Given the attitude of some male clergy within the Catholic wing of the Church of England to the ordination of women, it might be anticipated that women deacons who identified themselves with the Catholic wing would have experienced greater difficulty in finding a sympathetic training incumbent. The data give some support to this view.

Overall, the women deacons who described themselves as Catholics reported a less positive attitude toward their training incumbent than those who described themselves either as identifying with the middle way of Anglicanism or with the

Evangelical wing of Anglicanism. The strongest contrast, however, was between the Catholic women deacons and the Evangelical women deacons. For example, while 72% of the Evangelicals found their training incumbent to be generally helpful and constructive, the proportion dropped to 66% among the Catholics. While 17% of the Evangelicals considered that their training incumbent felt uncomfortable working with a female colleague, the proportion rose to 24% among the Catholics. While 29% of the Evangelicals reckoned that their training incumbent felt threatened by them, the proportion rose to 35% among the Catholics.

These statistics suggest that life may have been tougher for Catholic women deacons than for Evangelical women deacons. While those within the Catholic wing of the Church of England who opposed the ordination of women were busy marshalling their case, perhaps those Catholic Anglicans who supported the ordination of women should have been sharing more active concern for those Catholic women already exercising the ministry of the diaconate.

Are non-stipendiaries different?

Intuition might suggest that the stipendiary and the non-stipendiary curates would experience rather different qualities of relationships with their training incumbents, for at least three reasons. To begin with, the training incumbent may be responsible for shaping much of the working life of the stipendiary curate, while for many non-stipendiary curates a significant part of their lives is shaped apart from their parochial ministry. Second, it may be suspected that stipendiary clergy, or career clergy, may be seeking a rather different quality of training and support than their non-stipendiary colleagues. Third, while stipendiary clergy are generally directed to training parishes which have specific needs or expectations regarding assistant clergy, non-stipendiary clergy are not infrequently licensed to parishes in which they already live or which are near to their established home.

The data from the survey, however, support none of these arguments for a marked difference in the relationship with the training incumbent enjoyed by stipendiary women deacons and by non-stipendiary women deacons. For example, 70% of the non-stipendiary women deacons and 69% of the stipendiary women deacons found their training incumbent generally helpful and constructive.

Similarly, 18% of the non-stipendiary women deacons and 17% of the stipendiary women deacons considered that their training incumbent felt uncomfortable working with a female colleague, while 28% of non-stipendiary and 31% of stipendiary women deacons considered that their training incumbent felt threatened by them.

Hearing the stories

Listening to the personal stories told by the women deacons about the experience of working with their training incumbent highlights five main issues.

First, when the relationship with the training incumbent went wrong, this could leave scars which lasted for many years and restricted future ministry. One woman wrote as follows.

> I feel that having an unsupportive first incumbent has been highly detrimental: dampening enthusiasm and restricting outlets for my ministry. *(stipendiary, cathedral clergy aged 28)*

Another woman said quite strongly:

> I was ordained in 1987 and appointed as curate. Left stipendiary ministry in 1990 (difficulty with incumbent). *(secular employment aged 51)*

Second, listening to the stories, it became plain that some training incumbents were ill equipped for managing junior colleagues. One woman described her training incumbent as a manic depressive whose reactions she found unstable and unreliable. Another woman deacon found herself at the mercy of a priest who bullied her.

> My first incumbent started with enthusiasm, but after several years our relationship ended disastrously because he bullied me unmercifully. *(non-stipendiary, parish deacon aged 50)*

Third, many women deacons faced the problem of working with a male priest who opposed the ordination of women. For some women the experience was debilitating.

> First appointment: very satisfied with parish and ministry but very dissatisfied with my incumbent who opposed the ministry of women and was very unsupportive. *(stipendiary, parish deacon aged 43)*

Other women were more successful and effected a shift in their incumbents' attitude, as illustrated by the following comment.

> The last incumbent started out madly anti women deacons before I was made a deacon but has entirely changed his views and was a tremendously good trainer - but wouldn't share preaching (which he himself did very well). *(non-stipendiary, parish deacon aged 59)*

Fourth, there were training incumbents who were either not interested in or simply not equipped to act as trainers. One woman wrote as follows.

> Help of first incumbent - virtually none except by example which was excellent on sacraments, pastoring, spiritual direction and visiting. *(stipendiary, parish deacon aged 59)*

Another woman made the following comment.

> I surprised myself by saying my incumbent was very supportive, and then struggled to think of concrete ways in which he had helped develop my ministry. In hindsight, his support appears to be more of the encouragement to try new things or space to exercise and develop gifts rather than active help. *(stipendiary, parish deacon aged 38)*

Fifth, some women deacons told the tale of being directed to their first parish as deacon, not to benefit from the quality of training which the parish could provide, but to respond to the needs of that parish. A clear example is provided by the following extract.

> I was a parish worker before being ordained a deacon. I was asked to go to work with a difficult incumbent after being ordained deacon because they couldn't put a curate to work with such a difficult person. My faith and years of experience seemed the grounds for asking me to take on the difficult appointment. *(stipendiary, deacon in charge aged 57)*

These accounts raise questions about the processes of the selection and training of training incumbents and the continuing monitoring and support provided for the relationship between training incumbent and curate.

5 Last appointment as deacon

Introduction

One of the major problems facing women deacons within a church which refused to ordain women to the priesthood concerned the lack of promotional opportunities. Having served a first curacy under the supervision of a training incumbent, many of the more mature male candidates could begin to hope for an appointment in which they could have sole charge of their own church and parish. On the other hand, the women who wished to remain in parish ministry after serving their training curacy would still tend to find themselves responsible to a male incumbent, continuing to work either as a senior assistant curate, as a parish deacon, or as a member of a team ministry.

This chapter sets out to explore the extent to which the frustrations experienced during the training curacy extended into the later phase of ministry by inviting the women deacons to reflect on their last appointment as deacon. How many of the women deacons felt that their last incumbent, when they were still in deacon's orders, gave them an *equal* share of the responsibility in parish ministry? Or how many now felt properly included at that stage in ministry by their incumbent in making parish decisions? While still deacons, how many women felt that their last incumbent failed to delegate sufficient aspects of ministry to them? Or how many felt exploited by having too much work delegated to them? While still deacons, to what extent did the women feel that sufficient use was being made of their talents by their last incumbent? Or to what extent did they feel that they were being properly supported by adequate feedback?

Overview

The survey results reveal two main trends. On the one hand, there had been some real improvement in the experiences of women deacons between their first appointment and their last appointment as deacon. For example, while during their first appointment 32% of the women deacons felt that an inadequate range of tasks had been delegated to them, the proportion fell to 24% who felt this way about their last appointment as deacon. Similarly, the proportion of women deacons who felt that they had been given an equal share of responsibility in parish ministry rose from 36% during their first appointment to 44% in their last appointment as deacon.

Table 5 Last appointment as deacon

	Yes %	? %	No %
My last incumbent as deacon:			
did not delegate enough tasks to me	24	10	66
delegated too many tasks to me	10	11	80
did not make sufficient use of my talents	28	10	63
did not give me sufficient feedback	31	10	59
included me in making parish decisions	65	11	24
gave me an equal share of the responsibility	44	14	42

On the other hand, in other areas improvements in the experiences of the women deacons had been more marginal. For example, the proportion of the women deacons who felt that they had been properly included in making parish decisions rose only slightly from 62% during their first appointment to 65% in their last appointment as deacon. Similarly, the proportion of the women deacons who felt that insufficient use was made of their talents in ministry fell only slightly from 32% during their first appointment to 28% in their last appointment as deacon. The proportion of the women deacons who felt that they were being given insufficient feedback by their incumbent fell from 40% during their first appointment to 31% in their last appointment as deacon.

At a conservative estimate, these statistics indicate that before the opportunity of priesting was offered to them, between one in four and one in three women deacons felt that her talents were being inadequately or inappropriately deployed in ministry. This could be seen as an enormous waste of the church's resources and as an unfair burden on women deacons themselves.

Does age make a difference?

The women deacons who were least content with their last appointment as deacon were those in the oldest age group, aged sixty or over. These were the women whose ministry was nearing its end and for whom time was already slipping away. Having served as deacons under male incumbents, they seem to have been becoming especially restless with a form of ministry which denied to them the opportunities available to their male colleagues. The contrast is most clear when the perceptions of the women deacons aged sixty or over are compared with the perceptions of the women deacons under forty years of age. These younger women, with twenty or thirty more years of ministry ahead of them, hold the most positive view of their last appointment as deacon.

While 21% of the women deacons under the age of forty complained that their last incumbent, while they remained in deacon's orders, did not delegate enough tasks to them, the proportion rose to 28% of the women deacons aged sixty or over. While 20% of the women deacons under the age of forty complained that their last incumbent, while they remained in deacon's orders, did not make sufficient use of their talents, the proportion rose to 33% among those aged sixty or over. While 27% of the women deacons under the age of forty complained that their last incumbent, while they remained in deacon's orders, did not give them sufficient feedback, the proportion rose to 32% among those aged sixty or over.

While 71% of the women deacons under the age of forty considered that their last incumbent, while they remained in deacon's orders, included them in making parish decisions, the proportion fell to 60% among those aged sixty or over. While 45% of the women deacons under the age of forty considered that their last incumbent, while they remained in deacon's orders, gave them an equal share of the responsibility, the proportion fell to 39% among those aged sixty or over.

On the other hand, while 12% of the women deacons under the age of forty complained that their last incumbent, while they remained in deacon's orders, delegated too many tasks to them, the proportion fell to 7% among those aged sixty or over. The complaint among the older women deacons is not that they had too much to do, but that they had too little to do. As they experienced the situation, their talents and their ministry were not being put to the best effect.

Does marital status make a difference?

Generally the experiences of the single and the married women deacons were very similar in their last appointment as deacons. The women deacons who were least satisfied with their last appointment as deacon were those who had been widowed. The contrast is seen most clearly when the perceptions of the widowed women deacons are compared with the perceptions of the married women deacons.

The widowed women deacons were more likely than the married women deacons to feel that their last incumbent, while they remained in deacon's orders, did not delegate enough tasks to them (36% compared with 23%). The widowed women deacons were less likely than the married women deacons to feel that their last incumbent, while they remained in deacon's orders, delegated too many tasks to them (5% compared with 11%). These figures clearly suggest that the widowed women deacons were anxious for more to do in the parish at that stage in their ministry.

While 25% of the married women deacons felt that their last incumbent, while they remained in deacon's orders, did not make sufficient use of their talents, this was the case for 45% of the widowed women deacons. While 28% of the married women deacons felt that their last incumbent, while they remained in deacon's orders, did not give them sufficient feedback, this was the case for 50% of the widowed women deacons.

At the same time, only 43% of the widowed women deacons felt that their last incumbent, while they remained in deacon's orders, included them in making parish decisions, compared with 68% of the married women deacons. Only 36% of the widowed women deacons felt that their last incumbent, while they remained in deacon's orders, gave them an equal share of responsibility, compared with 45% of the married women deacons.

Taken overall, these statistics draw attention to the particular problems of women deacons who had lost their partner. These were the women who had time and energy to invest in parishes which seemed unable to welcome what they had to offer. These were the women who had come face to face with their own mortality through the death of their husband and were anxious to make the most of their remaining ministry within a church which seemed unable to receive what they were wanting to give.

While the divorced women deacons were considerably less content than the married women deacons in their first appointment, the difference is less pronounced in their last appointment as deacon. For example, 22% of the divorced women deacons and 23% of the married women deacons complained that their last incumbent, while they remained in deacon's orders, did not delegate enough tasks to them, while 9% of the divorced women deacons and 11% of the married women deacons complained that their last incumbent, while they remained in deacon's orders, delegated too many tasks to them.

On the other hand, the divorced women deacons still felt less included in some aspects of parish life than the married women deacons. For example, the divorced women deacons were less likely than the married women deacons to feel that their last incumbent, while they remained in deacon's orders, included them in making parish decisions (59% compared with 68%). The divorced women deacons were less likely than the married women deacons to feel that their last incumbent, while they remained in deacon's orders, gave them an equal share of the responsibility (41% compared with 45%). The divorced women deacons were more likely than the married women deacons to feel that their last incumbent, while they remained in deacon's orders, failed to give them adequate feedback (37% compared with 28%).

Taken overall these statistics indicate that ministry was more difficult for divorced women deacons.

Does church tradition make a difference?

While church tradition made a considerable impact on the initial response to God's call to ordination, the impact of church tradition was much less discernable in the first appointment. The statistics in the present section demonstrate that by the time of their last appointment as deacon, there were hardly any differences at all between the perceptions of women deacons on the Catholic wing and on the Evangelical wing of the church.

For example, 26% of the Catholics and 25% of the Evangelicals complained that their last incumbent, while they remained in deacon's orders, did not delegate enough tasks to them. At the same time, 10% of the Catholics and 11% of the Evangelicals complained that their last incumbent, while they remained in deacon's orders, delegated too many tasks to them. The same proportions of Catholic and Evangelical deacons considered that their last incumbent, while they remained in deacon's orders, gave them an equal share of the responsibility (43% and 43%). Similar proportions of Catholic and Evangelical deacons considered that their last incumbent, while they remained in deacon's orders, included them in making parish decisions (67% and 65%).

The only significant difference between the Catholics and the Evangelicals concerned their perceptions of the feedback received from their incumbent. This time it was the Evangelicals who were more likely than the Catholics to complain that their last incumbent, while they remained in deacon's orders, did not give them sufficient feedback (35% compared with 30%).

Once again the response of the women deacons who identified with the middle way of Anglicanism toward their last appointment as deacon did not differ significantly from the overall response of all the women deacons considered together.

Are non-stipendiaries different?

In their last appointment as deacon the experiences of the non-stipendiary women deacons remained significantly different from the experiences of the stipendiary women deacons. Generally, the non-stipendiary women deacons felt less included in parish life than was the case for their stipendiary colleagues. This is demonstrated by the fact that, while 70% of stipendiary women deacons feel that their last incumbent, while they remained in deacon's orders, included them in making parish decisions, the proportion fell to 61% among non-stipendiary women deacons. While half of the stipendiary women deacons felt that their last incumbent, while they remained in deacon's orders, gave them an equal share of the responsibility (48%), the proportion fell to one third among the non-stipendiary women deacons (34%).

The non-stipendiary women deacons also felt less fully deployed and valued than was the case for their stipendiary colleagues. This is demonstrated by the fact that more non-stipendiary than stipendiary women deacons were likely to complain that their last incumbent, while they remained in deacon's orders, had not delegated enough tasks to them (28% compared with 23%). More non-stipendiary than stipendiary women deacons were likely to complain that their last incumbent, while they remained in deacon's orders, failed to give them sufficient feedback (37% compared with 30%).

Given the general deployment strategy of the Anglican church, non-stipendiary priests as much as non-stipendiary deacons are likely to remain in a secondary role, with responsibility to a stipendiary incumbent. The findings of the present survey should alert the church to the potential strains and dissatisfaction with this form of ministry.

Hearing the stories

The women deacons' reflections on their last appointment, while they remained in deacon's orders, highlight four important issues about the role of women in ministry during the period before the church ordained women to the priesthood.

First, when these women deacons proceeded to their second appointment, they remained as deacons. They did not conform to the usual pattern of diaconate followed by priesting. Their continuing role as deacons left clear constraints on the kind of post to which they could move after their first appointment. This is explained in different ways by two women deacons.

> If I had been male I would not have taken a second curacy. I feel constrained by still being a deacon and a curate, whilst those I trained alongside are now incumbents. *(stipendiary, parish deacon aged 32)*

> My first appointment changed into my second without my moving, largely because of the shortage of second posts. *(stipendiary, parish deacon aged 56)*

Second, the problems generated by this lack of second posts for women deacons were often compounded by the fact that many of these women deacons tended both to be older and to bring a wider range of experience to their ministry than many of their male counterparts. Their experiences both in ministry and more widely were not always reflected in their second and subsequent appointments, as is illustrated by this woman.

> I was not happy about coming to this parish and refused it once but was persuaded because my age was making it difficult to get another place. *(non-stipendiary, assistant curate aged 65)*

Third, a lot can depend for these women on the level of responsibility given to them by their incumbent. This level of responsibility can vary greatly from one woman deacon to another. Some women deacons felt that they had been given too little responsibility, as demonstrated by the following account.

> I am an NSM deacon who simply is not now involved in baptisms and only occasionally in weddings and funerals - mainly because of the churchmanship of my fairly new rector who feels the local priests should primarily do all these things. *(non-stipendiary, parish deacon aged 66)*

Conversely, there are other women deacons who felt that they had too much to deal with, as this woman says.

> Personally, I feel I have too many tasks/areas of ministry to cope with, thrown in too much at the deep end. *(stipendiary, team minister aged 28)*

However, still other women deacons felt that they had achieved a good balance with their incumbent.

> We work as colleagues - I run the daughter church which is in a clearly defined area. *(stipendiary, deacon in charge aged 39)*

It is clear that incumbents in such situations needed to be aware that this was not the woman deacon's first curacy and that they needed to be treated accordingly by recognition of their skills in ministry.

Fourth, problems associated with being part of a clergy couple during a first appointment are still present in subsequent appointments since there is no clear structure by which the church can deal with clergy in this situation. The experience of the following woman deacon found that moving together with her husband to another appointment exacerbated problems in her own ministry.

> When my husband moved to be rector of three country parishes, I became NSM parish deacon. The difference in parish population means all occasional offices are now taken by my husband and are expected to be. In my first parish I did many more. *(non-stipendiary, parish deacon aged 54)*

These accounts clearly illustrate the problems which were faced by women deacons moving from their first training appointment to a second appointment within a church which at that stage had failed both to accept the ordination of women to the priesthood and to develop appropriate structures to accommodate the effective ministry of permanent deacons.

6 Last incumbent as deacon

Introduction

For the deacon the question of the working relationship with an incumbent is generally as important during subsequent appointments as during the first curacy. There is, however, one very important difference at this later stage of ministry. Often initial appointments are made on an allocation basis and the individual curate may not have a range of opportunities from which to choose or be given much choice in where she is appointed to serve. Subsequent appointments often involve much more freedom of choice, with more opportunity for both incumbents and deacons to choose those with whom they will be working so closely in parish ministry. It is to be anticipated, therefore, that better working relationships will exist at later stages in ministry. It is also to be anticipated that fewer incumbents who felt uncomfortable working with women would have chosen a more senior woman colleague (unless working with a woman deacon previously helped to change how they felt about working with women in ministry).

This chapter sets out to explore, therefore, whether the women deacons perceived their relationship with their last incumbent as deacon to have been different from their relationship with their training incumbent. How many of the women deacons felt that their last incumbent, while they remained in deacon's orders, was generally unhelpful or unconstructive toward them? Or how many felt that their last incumbent, while they remained in deacon's orders, was uncomfortable working with a female colleague? To what extent did the women deacons perceive their last incumbent, while they remained in deacon's orders, felt threatened by them? Or to what extent did they perceive their last incumbent, while they remained in deacon's orders, to have been overprotective of them?

Finally this chapter examines the implications of the close working relationship between the male incumbent and the female colleague for the incumbent's wife and for the female colleague's partner.

Overview

Table 6 Last incumbent as deacon

	Yes %	? %	No %
My last incumbent as deacon:			
was generally helpful and constructive	74	11	16
felt uncomfortable working with a female colleague	12	13	76
felt threatened by me	22	16	62
was too protective of me	8	9	83
My last incumbent's wife felt threatened by me	10	18	72
My partner felt threatened by my last incumbent	5	7	88

The survey results show that overall the women deacons enjoyed a better level of relationship with their last incumbent, while they remained in deacon's orders, than with their training incumbent. At the same time, there remained a disadvantaged minority of women deacons who continued to feel that they failed to enjoy the best of working relationships with their last incumbent, while they remained in deacon's orders.

The most noticeable improvement concerned the women deacons' perceptions of their incumbent's attitude toward working with women. While 20% of the women deacons felt that their training incumbent was uncomfortable working with a female colleague, the proportion fell to 12% who felt that way about their last incumbent, while they remained in deacon's orders. While 32% of women deacons felt that their training incumbent was threatened by them, the proportion fell to 22% who felt that way about their last incumbent. While

11% of the women deacons felt that their training incumbent was too protective of them, the proportion fell to 8% who felt that way about their last incumbent.

There was a significant improvement in the proportion of the women deacons who felt that they posed a threat to their incumbent's wife, from 20% who thought this way *vis à vis* their first incumbent's wife to 10% who thought this way about their last incumbent's wife. On the other hand, while 6% of the women deacons recognised that their partner felt threatened by their first incumbent, 5% still felt the same way about their last incumbent, while they remained in deacon's orders.

While overall 19% of the women deacons felt that their training incumbent was generally unhelpful and unconstructive toward them, 16% still felt the same way about their last incumbent, while they remained in deacon's orders.

At a conservative estimate, these statistics indicate that before the opportunity of priesting was offered to them, between one in ten and one in five women deacons felt that the working relationship with her last incumbent was quite unsatisfactory.

Does age make a difference?

The experience of the four cohorts of women deacons (those under the age of forty, those in their forties, those in their fifties and those aged sixty or over) regarding the last incumbent with whom they served, while they remained in deacon's orders, were all very similar. Nevertheless, some contrasts emerged between the cohorts which deserve comment.

The age cohort with the least positive attitude toward their last incumbent, while they remained in deacon's orders, was the women deacons in their fifties. The age cohort with the most positive attitude toward their last incumbent, while they remained in deacon's orders, was the women deacons under the age of forty. The following statistics illustrate the contrast between these two age groups.

While eight out of every ten (79%) of the women deacons aged under forty found the last incumbent with whom they served in deacon's orders generally helpful and constructive, the proportion fell to seven out of every ten (70%) of the women deacons in their fifties. While 7% of the women deacons aged under forty had concluded that the last incumbent with whom they served in deacon's orders felt uncomfortable working with a female colleague, the proportion doubled to 15% of the women deacons in their fifties. While 20% of the women deacons aged under forty considered that the last incumbent with whom they served in deacon's orders felt threatened by them, the proportion rose to 24% of the women deacons in their fifties.

Does marital status make a difference?

The attitudes of the married and single women deacons toward the last incumbent with whom they served in deacon's orders are in many ways very similar. For example, 20% of the married women deacons considered that the last incumbent with whom they served as deacons felt threatened by them, and so did 23% of the single women deacons. Similarly, 9% of the married women deacons considered that the last incumbent with whom they served as deacons was overprotective of them, and so did 7% of the single women deacons.

The only significant difference at this stage of ministry between the married and the single women deacons concerned their perceptions of their partner's attitude toward their incumbent. While 4% of the married women deacons considered their partner felt threatened by the last incumbent with whom they served as deacons, the proportion rose to 17% among the single women deacons. This finding may highlight the difficulty of maintaining close personal relationships in the context of parochial ministry.

The real issue focused by marital status, however, concerns the distinctive experience of the widowed women deacons at this stage of their ministry. This group of women deacons reports a much less positive attitude toward the last incumbent with whom they served as deacons than either their married or single colleagues. For example, while 76% of the married women deacons found that their last incumbent was generally helpful and constructive, the proportion fell to 60% of the widowed deacons. While 11% of the married women deacons considered that their last incumbent felt uncomfortable working with a female colleague, the proportion rose to 26% of the widowed women deacons. While one in five (20%) of the married women deacons had come to the conclusion that her last incumbent felt threatened by her, the proportion rose to one in three (33%) of the widowed women deacons.

The widowed women deacons were also more inclined to feel that their last incumbent's wife felt threatened by them than was the case among the married women deacons (14% compared with 10%).

In some ways the experiences of the divorced women deacons sits between the experiences of the married women deacons and the widowed women deacons. For example, 26% of the divorced women deacons considered that the last incumbent with whom they worked in deacon's orders felt threatened by them, compared with 20% of the married women deacons and 33% of the widowed women deacons. Similarly, 24% of the divorced women deacons considered that the last incumbent, with whom they worked in deacon's orders, felt uncomfortable working with a female colleague, compared with 11% of the married women deacons and 26% of the widowed women deacons.

Does church tradition make a difference?

The earlier chapter, concerned with the women deacons' experiences of working with their training incumbent, found significant differences between those working within the Catholic wing and the Evangelical wing of the church. Generally, the women deacons who described themselves as Evangelical reported a more positive experience of their training incumbent in comparison with the women deacons who described themselves as Catholic.

This difference between the experiences of those who describe themselves as Catholics and as Evangelicals remained true at this later stage in ministry, but to a less marked extent. For example, 76% of the women deacons who described themselves as Evangelicals found the last incumbent, with whom they served in deacon's orders, to be generally helpful and constructive, compared with 72% of the women deacons who described themselves as Catholics. Similarly, one in five (20%) of the women deacons who described themselves as Evangelicals considered that the last incumbent, with whom she served in deacon's orders, felt threatened by her, compared with one in four (24%) of the women deacons who described themselves as Catholics.

The experiences of the women deacons who described themselves as middle way Anglicans fell precisely between the experiences of the Catholics and the Evangelicals. For example, 74% of the women deacons who described themselves as middle way Anglicans found the last incumbent, with whom they served in deacon's orders, to be generally helpful and constructive, compared with 72% of the Catholics and 76% of the Evangelicals. Similarly, 22% of the women deacons who described themselves as middle way Anglicans considered that the last incumbent, with whom they served in deacon's orders, felt threatened by them, compared with 24% of the Catholics and 20% of the Evangelicals.

Are non-stipendiaries different?

The earlier chapter concerned with the women deacons' experiences of working with their training incumbent came to the somewhat surprising conclusion that there were few differences in the experiences of stipendiary and non-stipendiary deacons. The conclusion was surprising since intuition might suggest that stipendiary deacons and non-stipendiary deacons would relate to their training incumbent in somewhat different ways, for at least three reasons. Stipendiary deacons would be responsible to their training incumbent for a much larger part of their lives; stipendiary deacons would have more time available for the actual details of training; stipendiary deacons tend to move further away from their roots and established support mechanisms.

Very similar conclusions now emerge from contrasting the experiences of women deacons *vis à vis* the last incumbent with whom they worked while remaining in deacon's orders. The experiences of the two groups are almost identical. For example, 73% of the stipendiary women deacons found that the last incumbent, with whom they worked in deacon's orders, was generally helpful and constructive, and so did 73% of the non-stipendiary women deacons. One in eight (12%) of the stipendiary women deacons came to the conclusion that the last incumbent, with whom she worked in deacon's orders, felt uncomfortable working with a female colleague, and so did 12% of the non-stipendiary women deacons. One in ten (10%) of the stipendiary women deacons considered that the wife of the last incumbent, with whom she worked in deacon's orders, had felt threatened by her, and so did 10% of the non-stipendiary women deacons.

On the other hand, the stipendiary women deacons were more inclined than the non-stipendiary women deacons to consider that they posed some form of threat to the last incumbent with whom they served in deacon's orders. Thus, one in four (25%) of the stipendiary women deacons came to the conclusion that her last incumbent had felt threatened by her, compared with one in five (20%) of the non-stipendiary women deacons.

Hearing the stories

Listening to the personal stories told by the women deacons about experiences of working with their last incumbent, while they remained in deacon's orders, highlights three main issues.

First, a number of women deacons were still faced with the problem of working with a priest who was opposed to the ordination of women. For some women this resulted in limitations on their ministry.

> My actual parish work is very limited as my priest-in-charge is actively opposed to women clergy. *(non-stipendiary, chaplain aged 56)*

For some women the passing of the *Priests (ordination of women) Measure* exacerbated an already difficult situation. One woman wrote as follows.

> The vicar has refused to meet with me since the priesting vote, communicates by not telling me what to do, is barely civil when I speak to him. *(non-stipendiary, assistant curate/secular employment aged 34)*

Second, although it may seem unhelpful to both sides when women deacons were placed with incumbents who clearly did not support or agree with the ordination of women to the priesthood, there were many positive examples where working together has changed the mind of incumbents. One woman deacon, for example, witnessed a movement from opposition to declared acceptance.

> I have worked at many of these issues and there has been a change of attitude on his part from some opposition to the ordination of women to declared acceptance of this. *(stipendiary, parish deacon aged 56)*

Another woman expressed her experience as follows.

> My incumbent changed in his attitude from extremely cautious to supportive. *(stipendiary, team minister aged 52)*

Although changes in attitude can be effected, such changes seemed less likely to occur in situations where the incumbent was active in his opposition.

Third, it is clear that, when the relationship between the woman deacon and the incumbent was good, it gave strength to both the deacon and the incumbent, helping them both in their ministries.

> My current incumbent gives me the space and opportunity to develop in all areas of ministry, but as we work as equals it is difficult to define as help. *(stipendiary, parish deacon aged 41)*

Another wrote:

> I have an incumbent who is supporting, encouraging and caring. *(non-stipendiary, assistant curate aged 59)*

Fourth, traditionally the role of the incumbent's wife brought with it certain expectations in the parish. Such expectations can be upset by the presence of another female. For some women deacons this proved to be a real problem.

> The clergy relationships, vicar, his wife (also a deacon) and myself are indescribably painful and too complicated to enlarge upon. *(stipendiary, assistant curate aged 51)*

However, other women deacons discovered the potential for friendship and support from both their incumbent and their incumbent's wife.

> I have a wonderful rector and we get along very well. His wife and I are also good friends. *(stipendiary, assistant curate aged 33)*

Equally, the incumbent could find that he was in the minority, when the woman deacon and his own wife conspired against him. One women deacon put the issue this way.

> Additional question...Do you and your incumbent's wife gang up on your incumbent and make him feel threatened? *(non-stipendiary, assistant curate/secular employment aged 45)*

7 Clerical colleagues

Introduction

While in many ways the parochial structure encourages a sense of autonomy among the clergy within their own parish, there are other ways in which the Church of England encourages a greater sense of collegiality among the clergy at both deanery and diocesan levels. For many years clergy chapters had been constituted as organisations for men only. While the parishes in which the women deacons were working might have demonstrated an openness to accepting women in ministry, there is no guarantee that such openness extended to the whole of the wider clergy chapter. So how did the women deacons experience their reception by their clerical colleagues?

This chapter sets out, therefore, to assess the relationship between the women deacons and their clerical colleagues. How much did the women deacons really feel part of the professional life of other clergy in their area? To what extent did they experience trouble with some of their colleagues? Or to what extent did they feel that their clerical colleagues were really supportive of them?

How many of the women deacons were conscious of their clerical colleagues being unhappy when they took up their last appointment as deacons specifically because they were women? To what extent did they sense that their clerical colleagues' attitude toward women in ministry changed as a result of their own ministry in their area?

Overview

The survey results show that only a little over half of the women deacons felt part of the professional life of the clergy in their area (56%). One in every four (26%) clearly felt excluded from the professional life of the clergy in her area, and a further one in every five (19%) felt at best on the edge of that world.

Table 7 Clerical colleagues

	Yes %	? %	No %
I feel part of the professional life of other clergy in my area	56	19	26
I have trouble with some colleagues in my ministry position	43	10	47
My clerical colleagues are always very supportive of me	73	16	12
My clerical colleagues were unhappy when I took up my present appointment because I was a women	7	8	85
My clerical colleagues have become more favourable to women in ministry since my appointment	49	36	15

As many as four in every ten of the women deacons (43%) confessed to experiencing trouble with some colleagues, while a further one in every ten (10%) was unwilling to deny that this was the case. Slightly fewer than three quarters of the women deacons (73%) felt that they could always rely on their clerical colleagues for support.

A significant minority of the women deacons (15%) were suspicious that their clerical colleagues were unhappy when they took up their appointment because they were women; 7% found this reaction to be quite transparent, while a further 8% sensed that this was likely to have been the case.

However, half the women deacons (49%) found that clerical colleagues grew more favourable to women in ministry since their appointment. In contrast, 15% of the women deacons were clear that they had not sensed a positive change in colleagues' attitudes since their appointment. In other words, experience of a woman deacon as a clerical colleague may have been one of the best commendations for women in ministry.

Does age make a difference?

There is a very clear relationship between age and the way in which the women deacons experienced their relationship with clerical colleagues. Generally, the older women deacons held a much more positive view of their relationship with clerical colleagues, compared with the view of the younger women deacons. This trend can be illustrated most clearly by comparing the attitudes of the youngest cohort (those under the age of forty) with the attitudes of the oldest cohort (those aged sixty or over).

Nearly two thirds (63%) of the women deacons aged sixty or over considered that they felt part of the professional life of other clergy in their area, compared with less than half (46%) of the women deacons aged under forty. Nearly half (46%) of the women deacons aged under forty reported that they had trouble with some colleagues in their ministry position, compared with less than a third (32%) of the women deacons aged sixty or over. Similarly, 78% of the women deacons aged sixty or over agreed that their clerical colleagues were always very supportive of them, compared with 72% of the women deacons aged under forty.

The trend underpinning the experiences of the four cohorts of women deacons (those under the age of forty, those in their forties, those in their fifties and those aged sixty or over) was illustrated very clearly by their response to the item 'My clerical colleagues have become more favourable to women in ministry since my ordination.' While 36% of the women deacons aged under forty agreed with the sentiment, the proportion rose to 46% of the women deacons in their forties, to 55% of the women deacons in their fifties, and to 60% of the women deacons aged sixty or over.

Does marital status make a difference?

In many ways married and single women deacons shared similar experiences of their clerical colleagues. For example,

73% of the single women deacons reported that their clerical colleagues were always very supportive of them, and so did 74% of the married women deacons. Similarly, 43% of the single women deacons said that they had trouble with some colleagues in their ministry position, and so did 41% of the married women deacons. One in fourteen (7%) of the single women deacons said that clerical colleagues were unhappy when she took up her last appointment as deacon, and so did 7% of the married women deacons.

On the other hand, the married women deacons were more likely than the single women deacons to feel part of the professional life of other clergy in their area (57% compared with 51%).

The widowed women deacons stood apart from the single, married and divorced women deacons in one particular way regarding their experiences of clerical colleagues. The widowed women deacons were much more likely to say that they felt part of the professional life of other clergy in their area. This is the case for 75% of the widowed women deacons, compared with 51% of the single women deacons, 53% of the divorced women deacons and 57% of the married women deacons.

The divorced women deacons also stood apart from the single, married and widowed women deacons in one particular way regarding their experience of clerical colleagues. The divorced women deacons were less likely to feel that their clerical colleagues were always very supportive of them. This was the case for 66% of the divorced women deacons, compared with 71% of the widowed women deacons, 73% of the single women deacons, and 74% of the married women deacons.

Does church tradition make a difference?

The women deacons who were aligned with the Catholic wing of the Anglican church and the women deacons who were aligned with the Evangelical wing of the Anglican church reported different perceptions of their relationships with clerical colleagues in three distinctive ways.

First, the women deacons who described themselves as Evangelicals were more likely to perceive their clerical colleagues as supportive than the women deacons who described themselves as Catholics. Thus, 77% of the Evangelicals felt that their clerical colleagues were always supportive of them, compared with 67% of the Catholics.

Second, in spite of feeling less supported by their clerical colleagues, the women deacons who described themselves as Catholics were more likely to feel part of the professional life of the clergy than the women deacons who described themselves as Evangelicals. Thus, 58% of the Catholics felt part of the professional life of other clergy in their area, compared with 53% of the Evangelicals.

Third, in spite of feeling less supported by their clerical colleagues, the women deacons who described themselves as Catholics were more likely to feel that they had a positive influence on the attitudes of their colleagues than the women deacons who described themselves as Evangelicals. Thus, 51% of the Catholics reported that their clerical colleagues had become more favourable to women in ministry since their own appointment, compared with 45% of the Evangelicals.

In this area the women deacons who identified themselves with the middle way of Anglicanism came closer to the experiences of the Catholics on some issues and closer to the experiences of the Evangelicals on other issues. On the one hand, 75% of the middle way women deacons and 77% of the Evangelical women deacons felt that their clerical colleagues were always very supportive of them, compared with 67% of the Catholic women deacons. On the other hand, 53% of the middle way women deacons and 51% of the Catholic women deacons felt that their clerical colleagues had become more favourable to women in ministry since their own appointment, compared with 45% of the Evangelical women deacons.

Are non-stipendiaries different?

There are three basic differences in the ways in which stipendiary and non-stipendiary women deacons experienced their clerical colleagues.

First, the stipendiary women deacons were more likely than the non-stipendiary women deacons to say that they felt part of the professional life of other clergy in their area (62% compared with 56%). This is clearly consistent with the way in which many non-stipendiary clergy may have less time and less opportunity to become identified with the professional life of the clergy within their local area.

Second, the stipendiary women deacons were more likely than the non-stipendiary women deacons to say that they had trouble with some colleagues in their ministry (47% compared with 36%). This is consistent with the way in which many non-stipendiary clergy may generally have less time to associate with other clergy and, as a consequence, may be less conscious of the views that other clergy take toward them.

Third, it is the non-stipendiary women deacons who were more likely than the stipendiary women deacons to feel that their clerical colleagues had become more favourable to women in ministry since they took up their appointment (54% compared with 45%). An explanation for this difference in the perception of the stipendiary and non-stipendiary women deacons may be found in the suggestion that non-stipendiary women deacons may have presented less of a threat to their stipendiary male colleagues and as a consequence may have become more readily accepted.

In spite of these three important areas of difference, the stipendiary women deacons and non-stipendiary women deacons were conscious of similar levels of support from their clerical colleagues. Thus, three quarters (74%) of the stipendiary women deacons felt that their clerical colleagues were always very supportive of them, and so did 76% of the non-stipendiary women deacons.

Clerical colleagues 113

Hearing the stories

When listening to the personal stories of the women deacons in relation to their clerical colleagues, four main issues emerge.

First, it is clear that the women deacons were frequently finding a mixed reaction. This is clearly put by one woman deacon who expressed:
> Extreme support from some, total alienation by others and the two responses are often happening at the same time. *(stipendiary, team minister aged 48)*

Second, non-acceptance of women in ministry sometimes led to feelings of hostility toward the individual, although often this was removed from those with whom women deacons worked on a day to day basis to those who were part of the wider clergy chapter. This experience is summed up by one woman deacon in the following way.
> The only opposition I have encountered during my ministry has come from two of the neighbouring clergy in my present parish, one of whom will shortly be leaving the Church of England. *(stipendiary, deacon in charge aged 53)*

Another woman deacon drew attention to the way in which the clergy chapter found itself divided between those supporting and those rejecting the ministry of their female colleague.
> My own clergy colleagues are totally supportive but neighbouring parish clergy now have a problem with joint services. *(non-stipendiary, assistant curate aged 54)*

Third, although in theory some clerical colleagues accepted and supported women in ministry, it did not always come easily to them when faced with the reality of working together. There was need for adjustment to the change which might not necessarily have been anticipated by either side.
> I'm the first assistant curate for ages, attached to the rector of the team. My clergy are in theory and practice pro women priests, yet, I've had lots of strange comments which show

> some feelings of threat or lack of understanding. *(stipendiary, assistant curate aged 53)*

This extract illustrates how the appointment of a woman deacon may have opened up problems for male clergy that they had previously been able to ignore.

Fourth, there were also many positive comments illustrating the fruitful collaboration between men and women in ministry. One woman deacon summed up this positive benefit in the following way.

> My team colleagues and I have mutual support for one another and work very closely together. *(stipendiary, team minister aged 52)*

Another woman deacon illustrated how even clergymen who were not able to accept the ordination of women in theory, were nonetheless able to support and encourage the ministry of a woman deacon in practice.

> Of my eight Anglican colleagues only one objects to women priests. He is very pleasant and encourages my pastoral role. *(non-stipendiary, chaplain aged 57)*

8 Parishioners

Introduction

Throughout the period under consideration local churches remained very divided on the issue of the acceptability of women in ministry. While some congregations may have positively sought a woman deacon to join the ministry team, other congregations may have strongly resisted receiving a woman deacon. Inevitably some congregations were divided internally on this issue. To what extent did the women deacons find themselves working in churches where the ministry of women was fully acceptable, and how many of them experienced a lack of acceptance from the congregation?

As these women deacons were the first generation of women working in an *ordained* capacity within the Church of England, what changes did they see in the attitudes of their congregations as a consequence of their ministry? To what extent did the congregations become more favourable to women in ministry, or to what extent did attitudes become more hardened against women in ministry?

Finally, this chapter examines the broader issue regarding the general support the women deacons experienced from their congregation and parishioners. How supportive did they find their congregation? How much did they feel appreciated? How well did they feel accepted?

Overview

The survey results show that while slightly more than four out of every five of the women deacons were located in parishes where the ministry of women was fully acceptable (83%), nearly one in every five had a less positive experience. Thus, 5% of the women deacons clearly realised that their congregation was actually unhappy when they took up their appointment because they were women, while a further 13% suspected that this might have been the case.

Table 8 Parishioners

	Yes %	? %	No %
My congregation were unhappy when I took up my present appointment because I was a woman	5	13	83
My congregation have become more favourable to women in ministry since my appointment	69	23	8
My congregation are always supportive of me	84	13	3
I feel appreciated by most people in my ministry position	93	5	2
I feel accepted by most people in my ministry position	97	2	1

Even congregations which welcomed a woman deacon for the first time may have shared some apprehension about how this new form of ministry would work in practice. The overwhelming experience of the women deacons was that their ministry made a positive impact on the congregation. Seven out of every ten of the women deacons (69%) reported that their congregation had become more favourable to women in ministry since their appointment. Fewer than one in ten (8%) found that her ministry had clearly not achieved this effect on the congregation.

The majority of the women deacons felt most positive about their congregation and parishioners. Thus, 84% felt that their congregation was always supportive of them; 93% felt appreciated by most of the people to whom they ministered; 97% felt accepted by most of the people to whom they ministered.

While these figures do not encourage complacency, they suggest that the majority of women deacons were located in parishes which were ready to receive the ministry of women. Nonetheless, significant mistakes seem to have been made which may have been painful for the women deacons concerned, disruptive to the life of the local congregation, and detrimental to the general cause of women in ministry.

Does age make a difference?

Overall the oldest cohort of women deacons, those aged sixty or over, held a somewhat more positive view of their parishioners than the youngest cohort of women deacons, those aged under forty. The following statistics illustrate this point.

While four out of every five (79%) of the women deacons under the age of forty reported that their congregations were always supportive of them, the proportion rose to 87% of the women deacons aged sixty or over. While as many as 92% of the women deacons under the age of forty said that they felt appreciated by most people in their ministry position, the proportion rose to 97% of the women deacons aged sixty or over.

The older women deacons were also more likely than the younger women deacons to consider that they had made a positive impact on the attitudes of their congregation. Thus, while 64% of the women deacons aged under forty considered that their congregation had become more favourable to women in ministry since their appointment, the proportion rose to 72% of the women deacons aged sixty or over.

The women deacons in their forties occupy a midway position between the views of those under the age of forty and those aged sixty or over. For example, 84% of the women deacons in their forties reported that their congregation were always supportive of them, compared with 79% of the women deacons under the age of forty and 87% of the women deacons aged sixty or over. Similarly, 69% of the women deacons in their forties felt that their congregation had become more favourable to women in ministry since their appointment, compared with 64% of the women deacons under the age of forty and 72% of the women deacons aged sixty or over.

Does marital status make a difference?

The attitudes of the married women deacons and the single women deacons toward their parishioners were very close. For example, seventeen in every twenty (85%) of the single women deacons reported that their congregation were always supportive of them, and so did 85% of the married women deacons. Nearly seven in every ten (68%) of the single women deacons felt that their congregation had become more favourable to women in ministry since their own appointment, and so did 69% of the married women deacons. While 97% of the single women deacons felt accepted by most people in their ministry position, so did 97% of the married women deacons.

The widowed women deacons felt somewhat less supported by their parishioners than was the case among the single women deacons and among the married women deacons. Thus, four fiths (80%) of the widowed women deacons reported that their congregation was always supportive of them, compared with 85% of the single women deacons and 85% of the married women deacons. While 97% of the single women deacons and 97% of the married women deacons felt accepted by most people in their ministry position, the proportion, however, fell to 93% among the widowed women deacons.

The divorced women deacons felt somewhat less accepted by their parishioners than was the case among the single women deacons and among the married women deacons. Thus, 13% of the divorced women deacons said that their congregation were unhappy when they took up their present appointment because they were women, compared with 5% of the single women deacons and 4% of the married women deacons. While 85% of the married women deacons and 85% of the single women deacons felt that their congregation were always supportive of them, the proportion fell to 79% among the divorced women deacons.

Does church tradition make a difference?

The experiences of the women deacons on the Catholic wing of the church differed from the experiences of the women deacons on the Evangelical wing of the church in two ways.

On the one hand, the Catholic women deacons were a little less likely to have felt supported by their congregation than the Evangelical women deacons. While 86% of the Evangelical women deacons reported that their congregation were always supportive of them, the proportion fell a little to 82% among the Catholic women deacons. This view was also shared by 85% of the women deacons who identified with the middle way of Anglicanism.

On the other hand, the Catholic women deacons were a little more likely to feel that they had enhanced their congregation's attitude toward women in ministry. While 66% of the Evangelical women deacons reported that their congregation had become more favourable to women in ministry since their appointment, the proportion rose a little to 72% among the Catholic women deacons. This view was also shared by 71% of the women deacons who identified with the middle way of Anglicanism.

Church tradition bore no significant relationship with other perceptions in this section. For example, 6% of the Catholic women deacons, 5% of the Evangelical women deacons and 4% of the middle way women deacons felt that their congregation were unhappy when they took up their present appointment because they were a woman. At the same time, 93% of the Catholic women deacons, 93% of the Evangelical women deacons and 94% of the middle way women deacons felt appreciated by most people in their ministry position.

Are non-stipendiaries different?

The stipendiary women deacons and the non-stipendiary women deacons shared very similar experiences regarding their congregations and parishioners. For example, 4% of the non-stipendiary women deacons said that their congregation were unhappy when they took up their present appointment and so did 6% of the stipendiary women deacons. Similarly, 72% of the non-stipendiary women deacons found that their congregation became more favourable to women in ministry since their appointment, and so did 72% of the stipendiary women deacons.

The feeling of being appreciated by most people in their ministry position was reported by 93% of the non-stipendiary women deacons and by 95% of the stipendiary women deacons. The feeling of being accepted by most people in their ministry position was reported by 96% of the non-stipendiary women deacons and by 98% of the stipendiary women deacons.

Hearing the stories

Listening to the personal stories of the women deacons about their experiences with their congregations and with their parishioners highlights four main issues.

First, a number of women deacons drew a firm distinction between two groups of parishioners. Although many felt that the majority of their congregation accepted their ministry, they were also aware of a vocal minority who did not accept their ministry. One woman deacon made the point like this.

> 90% of the congregation may give good support but a vocal few object strongly. *(stipendiary, assistant curate aged 35)*

The presence of this vocal minority could make ministry difficult for some.

> There is a large majority for but a very vociferous minority against including one churchwarden and they have made my ministry very difficult. *(stipendiary, assistant curate aged 45)*

Second, opposition to the woman deacon's ministry by a minority could, in effect, restrict her ministry to all members of the congregation. One woman deacon took the conscious decision to respect the views of the minority and found that the majority failed to understand her approach to ministry.

> I live in a parish where the PCC did not wish to have a priestly ministry from me, so what I do in the parish is limited. Most of the congregation cannot understand this, but for the sake of unity within the parish I have limited my commitments. *(non-stipendiary, parish deacon aged 60)*

Third, although the women deacons in the present survey may have found acceptance of their diaconal ministry, there was still the clear recognition that this could change. This consideration was particularly relevant to some working within Anglo-Catholic parishes, as one woman wrote.

> An Anglo-catholic parish...before I arrived I suspect quite a lot of members of the congregation would have said they disagreed with the ordination of women to the priesthood. Now providing we aren't explicit about it, most of them treat me as if I were the parish priest. BUT the crunch has still to come, and perhaps half a dozen may still not accept that a eucharist celebrated by a woman is valid...I may well find myself facing a rejection of my ministry that I have not faced up to now. *(stipendiary, assistant curate aged 43)*

Fourth, stories told by many of the women deacons demonstrated that they found complete support from their congregations and full affirmation of their ministry. One woman put it as follows.

> I'm lucky to be working in a supportive congregation and ministry team; women are fully accepted and affirmed. *(non-stipendiary, parish deacon/secular employment aged 48)*

It is clear from many of the stories told by the women deacons that the church still needed to find ways of supporting women who found their ministry restricted by opposition from within their congregation. In such situations, as one woman pointed out, it was difficult to sort out a compromise with individuals when they would not communicate with you.

9 Family

Introduction

Ordained ministry has clear implications for home life and for family commitments. While one in three (34%) of the women deacons was single and a further 5% were divorced or separated, the majority (60%) were married. It is important to examine how married women deacons evaluated the effect of ministry on their family life. What proportion of married women deacons found their partner supportive of their ministry? Or what proportion of married women deacons found their partner resentful of the amount of time they spent in ministry?

There could also be a clear danger for some married women deacons that the demands of ministry might extend to encroach over the whole of life. To what extent is it the experience of the married women deacons that they often did not have enough time for their family?

Historically there has been the expectation that married Anglican priests are supported in their ministry by their wives. While economic and social factors have eroded the extent to which this expectation is met in practice, the image often still lives on. To what extent has this image now been transferred to the husbands of the married women deacons? How many married women deacons reported that their partner was active in their ministry?

Because the questions posed by this chapter are concerned solely with the experiences of the married women deacons, the present chapter follows a different pattern from other chapters in the book. The overview statistics are based solely on the responses of the married women deacons. Consequently, the section on marital status is omitted and the sections on age differences, church tradition and the comparison between stipendiary and non-stipendiary ministry are also based solely on the responses of the married women deacons.

Overview

Table 9 Family (married women deacons only)

	Yes %	? %	No %
My partner is very supportive of my ministry	96	2	2
My partner is very resentful of the amount of time I spend on my job	9	10	82
My partner is very active in my ministry	50	10	40
Often I do not have enough time for my family	52	13	35

The survey results show that the vast majority of married women deacons found that their partner was very supportive of their ministry (96%). By way of comparison, two married women deacons in every hundred (2%) reported that their partner was unsupportive of their ministry and a further two in every hundred (2%) preferred not to comment on this issue. The high level of support which married women deacons received for their ministry from their partner may reflect the care which is taken during the selection process to interrogate the wider context of family life.

While the majority of married women deacons found their partner supportive of their ministry, a warning is signalled by the proportion of married women deacons who were aware that their partner might be growing resentful of the amount of time they spent on the job. Almost one in five (19%) married women deacons was aware that this might be the case. While one in ten (9%) has recognised that this was already clearly the case, a further one in ten (10%) suspected that this might well be the case. The increase in marriage breakdown among male clergy may well offer a warning to women clergy.

The extent to which there was a danger for married women deacons to overwork is indicated by half of them (52%) recognising that they did not have enough time for their family.

The statistics demonstrate that the married women deacons were equally divided between those who found that their partner was actively involved in their ministry and those who found that this was not the case. Thus, 50% of the married women deacons reported that their partner was very active in their ministry, 40% reported that their partner was not active in their ministry and the remaining 10% kept an open verdict on the matter.

Does age make a difference?

Comparison of the four age cohorts (the married women deacons under the age of forty, those in their forties, those in their fifties, and those aged sixty or over) demonstrates how the pressures shifted over the period of the family life cycle. Three main trends emerge.

First, the youngest and the oldest cohorts shared much in common at these two periods in the family life cycle when the pressures seemed to have been at their lowest. For example, 99% of the married women deacons under the age of forty felt that their partner was very supportive of their ministry and so did 97% of the married women deacons aged sixty or over. Over half (54%) of the married women deacons under the age of forty felt that their partner was very active in their ministry and so did 54% of the married women deacons aged sixty or over. Similarly, 44% of the married women deacons under the age of forty made the point that often they did not have enough time for their family, and so did 43% of the married women deacons aged sixty or over.

Second, the pressures on family time were greatest among the married women deacons in their forties. While 44% of the married women deacons under the age of forty found that they often did not have enough time for their family, the proportion rose to 58% among those in their forties. The proportion then fell slightly to 53% among married women deacons in their fifties and returned to 43% among those aged sixty or over.

Third, the pressures on their partners' involvement in their ministry were greatest among the married women deacons in their fifties. While 54% of the married women deacons under the age of forty found that their partner was very active in their ministry, the proportion fell a little to 51% among the married women deacons in their forties and then fell further to 46% among the married women deacons in their fifties. The level returned to 54% among the married women deacons aged sixty or over.

Does church tradition make a difference?

The major relationship between church tradition and family life concerns the extent to which the married women deacon's partner was active in her ministry. The married women deacons who identified with the Evangelical wing of the church were much more likely to report that their partner was active in their ministry than was the case among the married women deacons who identified with the Catholic wing of the church. Thus, three in every five (62%) Evangelical married women deacons reported that their partner was very active in their ministry, compared with two in every five (40%) of the Catholic married women deacons. The married women deacons who identified with the middle way of Anglicanism occupied a midway position, with 51% of the middle way married women deacons reporting that their partner was very active in their ministry.

The second significant relationship between church tradition and family life concerns the perceived pressure on time for the family itself. The married women deacons who identified with the Catholic wing of the church felt greater pressure on the time available for family life than was the case among married women deacons who identified with the Evangelical wing of the church. At the same time, the married women deacons who identified with the Evangelical wing of the church felt greater pressure on the time available for family life than was the case among married women deacons who identified with the middle way of Anglicanism. Thus, 55% of the Catholic married women deacons reported that often they did not have enough time for their family, compared with 51% of the Evangelical married women deacons and 47% of the middle way married women deacons.

In spite of these two important areas of difference, very high proportions of the married women deacons from all three church traditions affirmed that their partners were very supportive of their ministry (94% of Catholic, 96% of middle way and 97% of Evangelical married women deacons). A minority of married women deacons from all three church traditions felt that their partner was very resentful of the amount of time they spent on their job (10% of Catholic, 6% of middle way and 8% of Evangelical married women deacons).

Are non-stipendiaries different?

The major distinction between the views of the stipendiary married women deacons and the non-stipendiary married women deacons concerns their perceptions of the pressures on the time available for their family. The married women deacons engaged in stipendiary ministry reported a significantly higher level of pressure on the time available for their family. Thus, 62% of the stipendiary married women deacons said that often they did not have enough time for their family, compared with 46% of the non-stipendiary married women deacons.

The second significant distinction between the views of the stipendiary married women deacons and the non-stipendiary married women deacons concerns the extent to which their partners were actually engaged in their ministry. A higher proportion of the married women deacons engaged in non-stipendiary ministry reported active involvement of their partners in their ministry. Thus, 56% of the non-stipendiary married women deacons said that their partner was very active in their ministry, compared with 51% of the stipendiary married women deacons.

In spite of these two important areas of difference, very high proportions of married women deacons in both forms of ministry affirmed that their partners were very supportive of their ministry (95% of non-stipendiary and 98% of stipendiary married women deacons). A minority of married women deacons in both forms of ministry felt that their partner was very resentful of the amount of time they spent on their job (10% of non-stipendiary and 7% of stipendiary married women deacons).

Hearing the stories

The women deacons' personal stories of their family's support and involvement in their ministry reveal three main issues.

First, it is clear that, with the advent of women in ordained ministry the traditional family unit of the clergy had changed. The church now had clergy husbands as well as clergy wives. Traditionally a role has been associated with the clergy wife. How far this expectation carried over to the clergy husband was not yet clear. On the one hand, many women deacons reported that their partner was a great support to their ministry. The following woman deacon spoke on behalf of a number of others when she said that her:

> husband and children are very supportive. *(stipendiary, deacon in charge aged 39)*

On the other hand, some women deacons found that partners could be equally restrictive. This woman deacon clearly resented her husband's influence on her ministry.

> The biggest limitation on my ministry is a husband who won't move house. *(stipendiary, sector minister aged 48)*

Second, some of the single women deacons acknowledged that the way in which they conducted their ministry might well be different if they were not single. One single woman deacon raised the following question.

> Do I work unsocial hours because I have no partner to share them with? Or am I enabled to do so because I have no husband to complain!? *(stipendiary, assistant curate aged 45)*

Some of the single women deacons also found their ministry restricted by their single status. One woman deacon expressed the matter like this.

> Most of my single deacon friends find the lack of a husband restricting. *(stipendiary, parish deacon aged 39)*

Third, the different stages in the lives of their children also made a difference to the ministry of more married women deacons. One woman deacon made the following point.

> Size and age of families clearly affects both appointments of women and also the number and nature of tasks. *(non-stipendiary, parish deacon aged 46)*

In particular the influence of maternity leave on the life of the woman deacon and on her sphere of ministry seemed to have been an issue inadequately thought through by the church. There were examples of lack of understanding, sympathy and help. For example, clearly pressure was brought to bear on the married woman deacon who made the following point.

> There will be problems when we start a family. My incumbent has stated I may like to move on at such a time, he doesn't want six months or however long of me on maternity leave etc. and him therefore being short staffed. *(stipendiary, chaplain aged 29)*

For other women deacons, however, the situation had been flexible after having a child.

> I am working stipendiary part time. I was full time until I took maternity leave and chose to return part-time. *(stipendiary, parish deacon aged 31)*

The comments of these women deacons clearly underlined both the need for a clear policy on maternity leave and the need for such policies to be properly implemented.

10 Friends

Introduction

The demands of ordained life carry all kinds of implications for friendship patterns. For many churchgoers the local congregation provides an important framework for social life and for friendship networks. At one level, the ordained clergy are welcomed into this framework and are expected to develop lasting friendships. At another level, the ordained clergy are expected to maintain a proper professional distance and objectivity within the life of the local church. Then, after a period of time, clergy are expected to move to a fresh congregation and to leave behind ties to their former charge. At one level clergy may appear to be surrounded by a rich resource of friendship. At another level, they may remain lonely and isolated.

This chapter sets out to explore, therefore, the experiences of the women deacons regarding friendships. To what extent did they keep a clear separation between private life and ministerial duties? How difficult had it been for them to make friends with people in the parish?

To what extent did the women deacons look outside the parish for their close friends? Or to what extent were they still drawing on the pattern of friendship established prior to ordination?

Overview

The survey results show that the women deacons were fairly evenly divided between those who kept their private life and ministerial duties separate (42%) and those who allowed their private life and ministerial duties to merge (36%). The remaining 22% may have felt some uncertainty regarding the extent to which these two aspects of life interacted. These two different approaches to the relation between ministry and private life may lead to different opportunities and problems.

Table 10 Friends

	Yes %	? %	No %
I am able to keep my private life and ministerial duties separate	42	22	36
It is difficult for me to make friends with people in my parish	27	14	59
Most of my close friends are outside my parish	67	9	25
The majority of my close friends are people I knew before being ordained	60	9	32

Three out of five of the women deacons (59%) experienced no difficulty in making friends with people in their parish. These were the women deacons who might have run the risk of being worn down by the excessive demands of friendship in the parish. On the other hand, one in every four of them (27%) was clear that she found it difficult to make friends with people in the parish, while a further 14% suspected this to be the case. These were the women deacons who might have run the risk of being worn down by loneliness in the parish.

Although many of the women deacons did not find difficulty making friends with people in the parish, the majority of them (67%) regarded most of their close friends to be outside the parish. For 60% of the women deacons their close friends were people they already knew before ordination. Problems of isolation may come when the mobility experienced within ministry and the demands of the job make it difficult to maintain such friendships and the links began to wear thin.

Does age make a difference?

The ability to keep private life and ministerial duties separate fluctuated between the four age cohorts. The highest proportion of women deacons to maintain this separation was found among those in their fifties (48%). This was the cohort who might have been re-learning the importance of objective distance from the place of their pastoral work. The lowest proportion of women deacons to maintain the separation between private life and ministerial duties was found among those in their forties (35%). This was the cohort who might have found themselves more closely cemented into the local community by the needs and expectations of growing teenage children.

The ability to make friends with people in the parish developed steadily across the age cohorts. While one in three (33%) of the women deacons under the age of forty reported that she found it difficult to make friends with people in the parish, this proportion was reduced to 28% among the women deacons in their forties, to 25% among the women deacons in their fifties, and to one in five (21%) of the women deacons aged sixty or over.

Possibly as a consequence of the older age cohort finding it easier to make friends with people in the parish, there was also a steady decline across the age cohorts in the proportion of women deacons who claimed that most of their close friends were outside the parish. While three out of every four (74%) of the women deacons under the age of forty claimed that most of their close friends were outside the parish, the proportion fell to 67% among the women deacons in their forties and among those in their fifties, and to 59% among the women deacons aged sixty or over.

Although there was a tendency to find it easier to make friends locally with increasing age, it was the older women deacons who were more likely to have come to realise that their really close friendships remained with those where roots were put down before ordination. Thus, while 53% of the women deacons under the age of forty reported that the majority of their close friends were people whom they knew before being ordained, the proportion rose to 56% among the women deacons in their forties, and to 66% among the women deacons in their fifties and among those aged sixty or over.

Does marital status make a difference?

The distinction between being married and being single has quite an influence on the women deacons' patterns of friendship. The married women deacons are less likely than the single women deacons to be able to keep their private life and ministerial duties separate (39% compared with 45%). The married women deacons found it easier to make friends with people in the parish. While 33% of the single women deacons reported that they found it difficult to make friends with people in the parish, the proportion fell to 23% among the married women deacons. As a consequence, the married women deacons were less likely than the single women deacons to feel that most of their close friends were outside their parish (64% compared with 73%). Nonetheless, the same proportions (60%) of the married women deacons and the single women deacons considered that the majority of their close friends were people whom they knew before being ordained.

For the widowed women deacons there was a particular tendency to keep personal life and public ministry apart. Thus, 51% of the widowed women deacons said that they were able to keep their private life and their ministerial duties separate, compared with 45% of the single women deacons and 39% of the married women deacons.

The divorced women deacons were less likely to report that the majority of their close friends were people whom they knew before being ordained (54% compared with 60% of the single and 60% of the married women deacons). This difference in response might reflect the way in which divorce disrupted long standing roots and damaged established kinship patterns. At the same time, the divorced women deacons found it as difficult as the single women deacons to make friends with parishioners. Thus, 33% of the divorced women deacons and 33% of the single women deacons reported that they found it difficult to make friends with people in their parish, compared with 23% of the married women deacons.

Does church tradition make a difference?

Differences in attitude toward friendship between women deacons who identified with the Catholic wing of the Anglican church and women deacons who identified with the Evangelical wing of the Anglican church seem to reflect the fundamental differences in the concept of ministry fostered by these opposing orientations. The Catholic view maintained a greater distance between deacon and people, while the Evangelical view maintained a closer identity between minister and people.

Accordingly, a higher proportion of women deacons who described themselves as Catholics reported that they were able to keep their private lives and ministerial duties separate than was the case among the women deacons who described themselves as Evangelicals (45% compared with 36%). Similarly, a higher proportion of women deacons who described themselves as Catholics reported that most of their close friends were outside their parish than was the case among the women deacons who described themselves as Evangelicals (72% compared with 64%). At the same time, the women deacons who described themselves as Catholics reported that they found it somewhat more difficult to make friends with people in their parish than was the case among the women deacons who described themselves as Evangelicals (30% compared with 26%).

In spite of these clear differences roughly the same proportions of Catholics (60%) and Evangelicals (58%) agreed that the majority of their close friends were people whom they knew before being ordained.

The women deacons who described themselves as middle way Anglicans were close to the Catholics in some respects and close to the Evangelicals in other respects. The middle way Anglicans were close to the Catholics in their ability to keep their private life and their ministerial duties separate. This was the case for 47% of the middle way Anglicans and 45% of the Catholics, compared with 36% of the Evangelicals. On the other hand, the middle way Anglicans were close to the Evangelicals in their ability to make friends in the parish. Thus, 24% of the middle way Anglicans and 26% of the Evangelicals reported that they found it difficult to make friends with people in the parish, compared with 30% of the Catholics.

Are non-stipendiaries different?

Stipendiary and non-stipendiary ministers often have quite a different relationship with the parish in which they serve. Generally, non-stipendiary clergy minister close to where they lived before ordination and continue to occupy the same house. Generally, stipendiary clergy move further away from their previous home and occupy a house provided by and within the parish where they serve. These two very different styles of ministry are likely to be reflected in different friendship patterns.

Accordingly, non-stipendiary women deacons were much less likely than stipendiary women deacons to report that they found it difficult to make friends with people in their parish (20% compared with 34%). Non-stipendiary women deacons were also less likely than stipendiary women deacons to claim that most of their close friends were outside their parish (52% compared with 75%).

On the other hand, full-time exposure to ministry may have a greater influence on changing long term friendship patterns than the part-time exposure of some forms of non-stipendiary ministry. Thus a smaller proportion of stipendiary women deacons reported that the majority of their close friends were people whom they knew before being ordained than was the case among non-stipendiary women deacons (61% compared with 71%).

However, in spite of these differences, roughly the same proportions of stipendiary women deacons (39%) and non-stipendiary women deacons (37%) felt they were able to keep distance between their personal and professional lives.

Hearing the stories

Listening to the personal experiences of the women deacons about the importance of their friends highlights three main areas.

First, there was a sense in which friends could give support by providing a sense of perspective on ministry particularly when things were difficult. One woman deacon found friends helped her to keep positive about the situation despite the difficulties.

> Also the level of support and encouragement in personal relationships affects whether one's attitude remains positive despite the difficulties. *(stipendiary, team minister aged 41)*

Second, friendships could provide the support which was needed when things went wrong. As one woman deacon found, this was especially the case in times of sickness.

> My health broke down, I received surprisingly little help and support from the official church but a lot from friends and relatives. *(non-stipendiary, permission to officiate aged 45)*

However, it was important that such friendships were maintained and this could be difficult with a busy ministerial life.

> I needed far more preparation for living as a parish minister - especially in how to carve out time, friends, hobbies for oneself - than I ever had. *(non-stipendiary, sector minister aged 40)*

Third, there was the recognition that the absence of friends and the support network which they provide could lead to feelings of loneliness and isolation. This could be particularly acute when moving to a new area removed from established social networks, as one woman deacon acknowledged.

> If I am lonely it is because I have only been in my present post a year, and settling down takes time. My family and close friends are not nearby. *(stipendiary, team vicar aged 52)*

It is clear from these accounts that both clergy and parishioners should appreciate that time needs to be made for friends as they form an integral part of an important support network.

11 Collaborative ministry

Introduction

A number of commentators on the ministry style exercised by ordained women suggest that women deacons may prefer a more collaborative style of ministry than that exercised by clergymen. This chapter sets out to explore, therefore, the extent to which the women deacons were conscious of involving others in their ministry. To what extent did the women deacons feel that they took other people's views fully into consideration in shaping their ministry? To what extent did they find that it came naturally to delegate responsibilities to others?

While in many ways a collaborative style of ministry is often seen to facilitate and enable the local church to develop the ministry skills of the whole people of God, there may be hidden costs for those who are committed to this form of ministry. Those who wish to encourage collaboration may find themselves trying too hard to accommodate other people's points of view. At the same time, they may become easy targets for strong minded individuals who wish to influence the life of the local church.

To what extent, therefore, were women deacons conscious of allowing other people's ideas to shape their ministry? To what extent were they conscious of other people trying too hard to influence their ministry? Or to what extent did they feel that other people interfered too much in their ministry?

Overview

The survey results show that nearly three quarters of the women deacons (72%) were conscious of taking other people's views fully into account in shaping their ministry. Fewer than one in ten (8%) took the strong minded stance of shaping her ministry without taking other people's views fully into account. If listening to others is a sign of collaborative ministry, women deacons were clearly committed to this ministry style.

Table 11 Collaborative ministry

	Yes %	? %	No %
I take other people's views fully into consideration in shaping my ministry	72	20	8
I find it hard to delegate responsibility to others	9	11	80
I allow other people's ideas to shape my ministry	26	32	42
Other people try too hard to influence my ministry	9	17	74
Other people interfere too much in my ministry	6	11	83

At the same time, well over three quarters of the women deacons (80%) did not find it hard to delegate responsibility to others. Fewer than one in ten (9%) took the view that she found it hard to delegate responsibility to others. If delegating responsibility to others is a sign of collaborative ministry, women deacons were clearly committed to this ministry style.

While valuing the involvement of others, the majority of the women deacons felt that they remained properly in command of their own decisions. While one in four of the women deacons (26%) recognised that she allowed other people's ideas to shape her ministry, just 9% felt that other people tried too hard to influence their ministry. The proportion fell to 6% who felt that other people interfered too much in their ministry.

However, the minority of the women deacons who felt that other people were trying too hard to influence their ministry or interfere in their ministry should not be ignored. The statistics suggest that one in ten of the women deacons might have benefited from some support and training in how to deal with such external pressures.

Does age make a difference?

The commitment to a collaborative style of ministry remained basically stable across the four cohorts of women deacons (those under the age of forty, those in their forties, those in their fifties, and those aged sixty or over). Two significant shifts are, however, revealed by the data.

First, there is some evidence that the younger women deacons were more committed to accommodating other people's opinions than their older colleagues. Thus, 75% of the women deacons under the age of forty reported that they took other people's views fully into consideration in shaping their ministry, compared with 72% of the women deacons in their forties, 70% of the women deacons in their fifties, and 70% of the women deacons aged sixty or over.

Second, there was a marked decrease with age in the proportion of women deacons who reported that they allowed other people's ideas to shape their ministry. While 29% of the women deacons under the age of forty and 31% of the women deacons in their forties agreed that they allowed other people's ideas to shape their ministry, the proportions fell to 23% among the women deacons in their fifties, and to 16% among the women deacons aged sixty or over.

Another feature revealed by these data is that the women deacons in the two middle cohorts were more likely than the youngest and oldest cohorts to experience pressure from others trying to influence their ministry. Thus, 12% of the women deacons in their forties and 11% of the women deacons in their fifties reported that other people tried too hard to influence their ministry, compared with 7% of the women deacons aged under forty and 4% of the women deacons aged sixty or over.

Does marital status make a difference?

The attitudes of married and single women deacons toward collaborative ministry were really quite similar. For example, 73% of the single women deacons said that they took other people's views fully into consideration in shaping their ministry, and so did 71% of the married women deacons. One in four (25%) of the single women deacons said that she allowed other people's ideas to shape her ministry, and so did 27% of the married women deacons. One in ten (9%) of the single women deacons found it hard to delegate responsibility to others, and so did 9% of the married women deacons.

The main way in which the profile of the widowed women deacons differed from that of the married and single women deacons concerned their perception of the way in which others tried to influence their ministry. Thus, 15% of the widowed women deacons said that other people tried too hard to influence their ministry, compared with 8% of the single women deacons and 9% of the married women deacons.

The main way in which the profile of the divorced women deacons differed from that of the married and single women deacons concerned the difficulty they experienced in delegating responsibility to others. Thus, 15% of the divorced women deacons said that they found it hard to delegate responsibility to others, compared with 9% of the married and single women deacons.

Does church tradition make a difference?

Church tradition bears little relationship to the attitudes of the women deacons toward collaborative ministry. For example, 11% of the women deacons who described themselves as Catholics felt that other people tried too hard to influence their ministry, and so did 9% of the women deacons who identified with the middle way of Anglicanism and 8% of the women deacons who described themselves as Evangelicals. One in ten (10%) of the Catholics said that she found it hard to delegate responsibility to others, and so did 9% of the middle way Anglicans and 8% of the Evangelicals.

Such differences as occur in the responses are seen most clearly between the women deacons who described themselves as Catholics and the women deacons who described themselves as middle way Anglicans. In some ways the Catholics are more likely to endorse collaborative ministry styles. This point is illustrated by the way in which 28% of the Catholics said that they allowed other people's ideas to shape their ministry, compared with 23% of the middle way Anglicans and 25% of the Evangelicals. The point is also illustrated by the way in which 74% of the Catholics said that they took other people's views fully into consideration in shaping their ministry, compared with 70% of the middle way Anglicans and 71% of the Evangelicals.

Are non-stipendiaries different?

The data demonstrate that the non-stipendiary women deacons were slightly less committed to collaborative ministry than was the case among the stipendiary women deacons. This difference is illustrated by two key statistics. While 70% of the non-stipendiary women deacons said that they took other people's views fully into consideration in shaping their ministry, the proportion rose a little to 74% among the stipendiary women deacons. While 23% of the non-stipendiary women deacons said that they allowed other people's ideas to shape their ministry, the proportion rose to 29% among the stipendiary women deacons.

The stipendiary women deacons were more likely than the non-stipendiary women deacons to feel under pressure from others trying to influence their ministry. Thus, 11% of the stipendiary women deacons said that other people tried too hard to influence their ministry, compared with 7% of the non-stipendiary women deacons.

Hearing the stories

Listening to the personal experiences of the women deacons on the issue of collaborative ministry there is clearly a mixed reaction. The women deacons seem to fall into three distinct groups.

First, there were those who felt that women in holy orders bring a balance to ministry in that they are complementary to the existing ministry of men. One woman deacon made the point in the following way.

> Men and women are complementary in ministry. My colleague and I have different gifts and talents. *(stipendiary, parish deacon aged 42)*

Another woman noted simply that what really counted was her presence in the parish.

> It would appear that the value of my ministry in my previous appointment was predominantly in my being not my doing. The fact that I was there and available up front on Sundays and around the parish in the week made a lot of difference to folks. *(non-stipendiary, assistant curate aged 54)*

Second, there were those who felt that their ministry promoted a different response from their parishioners, which both men and women found helpful. One woman deacon pointed specifically to her distinctive ministry among women.

> At least on an individual basis, women have told me they find it easier to talk to a woman about women's things. *(stipendiary, assistant curate aged 50)*

Another woman deacon pointed specifically to her distinctive ministry among men.

> I find that men tell me very different things about themselves and their families compared with what they tell my male colleagues. *(non-stipendiary, parish deacon aged 59)*

Third, there seemed to be two distinct approaches to ministry reflected by the women deacons. Some women deacons felt that they were there to lead the parishioners.

> I see ordination and priesthood in terms of leadership and authority rather than in sacramental terms. *(stipendiary, parish deacon aged 44)*

Other women deacons felt that the role of women in ministry should be one of enabling others.

> Women in ministry should reflect the ministries of women in distinctive diaconal orders and laywomen as well as those aspiring to priesthood. I would hope women were trying to break down rather than collude with an hierarchical view of the church. *(stipendiary, assistant curate aged 44)*

Clearly ministry is conceived in different ways by different women deacons.

12 Stress in ministry

Introduction

Stress and burnout are topics of increasing concern within many of the caring professions, including those concerned with education, health and social welfare. The clerical profession is no exception to this trend. The aim of the present chapter, therefore, is to assess the extent to which women deacons were conscious of stress in ministry.

A major source of stress in ministry arises from setting unrealistic and unattainable expectations. To what extent, then, were women deacons conscious of imposing unrealistic expectations on themselves?

A major sign of stress in ministry occurs when ministry begins to take over the whole of life. To what extent, then, were women deacons conscious of no longer having time for their hobbies and interests? Or to what extent were they conscious of simply not having enough time for themselves?

A major consequence of stress is reflected in feelings of isolation and loneliness. To what extent, then, were women deacons conscious of feeling lonely and isolated in their ministry?

For women deacons another cause for stress might have arisen from the very nature of diaconal ministry, when the diaconate did not lead into priesthood. To what extent, then, did these women deacons feel constrained by the limits of their ministry position?

Overview

The survey results show that three out of every four of the women deacons (74%) were conscious of imposing unrealistic expectations on themselves, compared with only 13% who felt that they were realistic in their self expectations. If setting unrealistic expectations is a recognised cause of stress, many of the women deacons may have been putting themselves at risk.

Table 12 Stress in ministry

	Yes %	? %	No %
Often I impose unrealistic expectations on myself	74	13	13
Often I do not have enough time for my hobbies and interests	75	8	17
Often I do not have enough time for myself	72	9	19
I often feel lonely and isolated in my ministry	32	13	56
I feel constrained by the limits of my ministry position	45	16	39

A clear consequence of setting unrealistic expectations is the erosion of personal time and space so that hobbies and interests get squeezed out of life. Three out of every four of the women deacons (75%) recognised that they did not have enough time for their hobbies and interests. A similar proportion (72%) of the women deacons recognised that they often did not have enough time for themselves. If the erosion of personal time and space is a recognised indicator of stress, many of the women deacons appear to have been showing such signs.

As many as one in every three of the women deacons (32%) recognised that she often felt lonely and isolated in her ministry. If loneliness and isolation are further indicators of stress in ministry, the voices of these women deacons needed to be taken seriously.

The statistics indicate that the practical constraints of diaconal ministry may well have functioned as a significant cause for frustration and stress among this sample of women deacons. Nearly half of the women deacons (45%) made the point that they felt constrained by the limits of their ministry position.

Does age make a difference?

These data reveal four trends regarding the relationship between age and signs of stress among women deacons.

The first trend shows how with increasing age women in ministry gradually became more realistic about the expectations which they imposed upon themselves. Four out of every five (80%) of the women deacons aged under forty said that they often imposed unrealistic expectations on themselves. This proportion fell a little to 77% among the women deacons in their forties, and then continued to fall to 71% among the women deacons in their fifties and to 64% among the women deacons aged sixty or over. This still means, however, that two out of every three women deacons in the oldest cohort were remaining unrealistic about the expectations which they imposed on themselves.

The second trend shows that the greatest pressure on time fell on the cohort of women deacons in their forties. Four out of every five (81%) women deacons in their forties said that they often did not have enough time for their hobbies and interests, compared with 75% of the women deacons under the age of forty and 76% of the women deacons in their fifties. The biggest contrast, however, occurs between the women deacons in their forties and the women deacons aged sixty or over. While 81% of the women deacons in their forties said that they often did not have enough time for their hobbies and interests, the proportion fell to 63% among the women deacons aged sixty or over. While 75% of the women deacons in their forties said that they often did not have enough time for themselves, the proportion fell to 66% among the women deacons aged sixty or over.

The third trend shows that women deacons in their forties and fifties were more likely to experience loneliness and isolation in ministry than either their younger colleagues or their older colleagues. Thus, 33% of the women deacons in their forties and 34% of the women deacons in their fifties said that they often felt lonely and isolated in their ministry, compared with 29% of the women deacons under the age of forty and 27% of the women deacons aged sixty or over.

Finally, the age cohort least likely to have felt constrained by the limits of their ministry position were the women deacons aged sixty or over. Perhaps these were the women who were too close to retirement to be especially worried. By way of contrast, the age cohort most likely to feel constrained by the limits of their ministry position were the women deacons in their fifties. Perhaps these were the women who felt that, although they have ministry ahead of them, time was running short. Thus, 41% of the women deacons aged sixty or over and 48% of the women deacons in their fifties felt constrained by the limits of their ministry position, compared with 46% of the women deacons in their forties and 45% of the women deacons under the age of forty.

Does marital status make a difference?

A similar proportion of the single women deacons and of the married women deacons imposed unrealistic expectations on themselves (73% and 75% respectively). Similar proportions of the single women deacons and of the married women deacons felt constrained by the limits of their ministry position (46% and 44% respectively). The differences in experiences between the married women deacons and the single women deacons occurred in relationship to pressures of time and feelings of isolation.

The married women deacons displayed slightly higher levels of stress in terms of pressures of time. Thus, 77% of the married women deacons said that they often did not have enough time for their hobbies and interests, compared with 73% of the single women deacons. On the other hand the single women deacons displayed slightly higher levels of stress in terms of feelings of isolation. Thus, 34% of the single women deacons said that they often felt lonely and isolated in their ministry, compared with 28% of the married women deacons. These differences between the experiences of the single women deacons and the married women deacons is consistent with the view that being married can both add to some kinds of pressures and reduce other kinds of pressures. On the one hand, the spouse may provide companionship and consequently reduce feelings of isolation and loneliness. On the other hand, the spouse may create another set of demands and impose further pressures on time.

The widowed women deacons presented quite a different profile from the married women deacons in a number of ways. The widowed women deacons were less likely than the married women deacons to impose unrealistic expectations on themselves (66% compared with 73%). The widowed women deacons were less likely than the married women deacons to feel that they had insufficient time for hobbies and interests (64% compared with 77%) or for themselves (58% compared with 74%). The widowed women deacons were more likely than the married women deacons to feel lonely and isolated in their ministry (41% compared with 28%) and to feel constrained by the limits of their ministry (58% compared with 46%).

The divorced women deacons showed two signs of stress at higher levels than the married women deacons. They were more inclined to impose unrealistic expectations on themselves. They were more inclined to feel isolated. While nearly three quarters (73%) of the married women deacons felt that they often imposed unrealistic expectations on themselves, the proportion rose to four fifths (80%) among the divorced women deacons. While over a quarter (28%) of the married women deacons often felt lonely and isolated in their ministry, the proportion rose to 48% of the divorced women deacons.

Does church tradition make a difference?

In many ways the experiences of the women deacons who described themselves as Catholics were very close to the experiences of the women deacons who described themselves as Evangelicals. While 74% of the Catholics often imposed unrealistic expectations on themselves, so did 76% of the Evangelicals. Nearly three quarters (72%) of the Catholics and 73% of the Evangelicals said that they often did not have enough time for themselves.

The two significant differences between the Catholics and the Evangelicals concerned their feelings of isolation and constraint. On the one hand, a higher proportion of the Evangelicals said that they often felt lonely and isolated in their ministry (34% compared with 30%). On the other hand, a higher proportion of the Catholics said that they felt constrained by the limits of their ministry position (47% compared with 42%). In both of these areas the middle way Anglicans followed the profile of the Catholics. Thus, 30% of the middle way Anglicans often felt lonely and isolated in ministry; 47% of the middle way Anglicans felt constrained by the limits of their ministry position.

Are non-stipendiaries different?

To some the demands of non-stipendiary ministry may seem even more daunting than the demands of stipendiary ministry, since non-stipendiary ministry is often offered on top of the demands of other full-time employment and commitments. To others the demands of non-stipendiary ministry may seem less demanding than the demands of stipendiary ministry, being properly off-set and balanced by the secular commitments.

The present data suggest that the stipendiary women deacons reported slightly more indicators of stress than the non-stipendiary women deacons. For example, while 73% of the non-stipendiary women deacons often imposed unrealistic expectations on themselves, the proportion rose to 77% among the stipendiary women deacons. Similarly, while 75% of the non-stipendiary women deacons often did not have enough time for their hobbies and interests, the proportion rose to

80% among the stipendiary women deacons. While 71% of the non-stipendiary women deacons often did not have enough time for themselves, the proportion rose to 75% among the stipendiary women deacons.

Hearing the stories

The women deacons' stories demonstrate four areas which can clearly lead to stress in ministry.

First, juggling a number of roles with differing expectations imposed both by themselves and by other people around them caused practical difficulties, as this woman deacon points out.

> My problems are trying to manage a demanding diocesan job in two days a week and run a busy community church. *(stipendiary, deacon in charge aged 59)*

Other women deacons found the disparity was rather between balancing those tasks which were necessary but neither enjoyable nor rewarding with those tasks which they enjoyed and found rewarding.

> The disparity between what I think I should be doing, what gives me satisfaction and what I am actually doing is considerably exacerbated by my not being in charge of the parish. *(stipendiary, parish deacon aged 59)*

Second, the level of expectation placed on deacons by those in authority over them could lead to problems, particularly when such expectations were unrealistic. Unrealistic expectations could lead to feelings of inadequacy or failure, as this woman deacon's story demonstrates.

> Very recently the bishop told me he was disappointed that I was unable to sort a situation out (I was working in a church undergoing great turmoil). What an unrealistically high expectation he had of me. *(unemployed, deacon aged 52)*

Third, there clearly came a point for some women deacons when ministry had taken over their life leaving no room for anything else. One woman deacon, for example, recognised this problem and took time to learn to deal appropriately with it.

> I needed far more preparation for living as a parish minister, especially in how to carve out time for friends, hobbies and oneself. *(stipendiary, sector minister, aged 40)*

Other women deacons have not been as successful in recognising and dealing with this particular problem. For some this has had serious consequences, as exampled by this woman deacon who found her health suffered dramatically.

> My health broke down...I have received surprisingly little help and support from the official church. Reports on my ministry were good, but the stresses of my working conditions seem to have permanently damaged my health. *(non-stipendiary, permission to officiate aged 45)*

Fourth, the frustration of not being able to proceed to the priesthood clearly had a detrimental effect on the ministry of women in two main ways. On the one hand, there was the assumption of ordinary people that women deacons were able to fulfil all priestly functions.

> The frustrations of being a deacon are emphasised by parishioners and community who accept my ministry as a full ministry alongside all my male colleagues, but realising the church's limitations which, for the most part don't make sense to ordinary people. *(stipendiary, team minister aged 45)*

On the other hand, for the women deacons themselves there were the restrictions on the number of opportunities available to them for developing and growing in their ministry.

> Now few women are incumbents or in charge of parishes, for the majority there is not freedom to work as called by God. *(non-stipendiary, parish deacon aged 49)*

13 Satisfaction in ministry

Introduction

Recent strands of research on professional burnout make a clear distinction between stress and satisfaction. To experience stress in ministry does not necessarily imply a lack of personal satisfaction from ministry. Indeed, sometimes high levels of stress and high levels of personal satisfaction can go hand in hand. This chapter sets out, therefore, to explore the satisfaction in ministry experienced by the women deacons. Overall, how satisfied did these women feel with their work in the church?

Satisfaction in ministry may comprise a range of key components. Satisfaction can derive from the sense that something worthwhile is being accomplished. What proportion of the women deacons, then, really felt that they were accomplishing things in their ministry?

Satisfaction can derive from the sense that difficulties are being overcome and solutions to problems are being found. What proportion of the women deacons, then, really felt that they were being successful at overcoming difficulties within their ministry?

Satisfaction can derive from the sense of personal growth and development. Within the clerical profession the aspect of personal growth which may carry most significance is that of spiritual development. What proportion of the women deacons, then, really felt that they were growing spiritually in their ministry?

While the clerical profession is not well paid, the basic philosophy underpinning the clerical stipend is that clergy should be enabled to live without undue financial anxiety and worry about money. To what extent were the women deacons satisfied with the level of remuneration which they received for their ministry?

Overview

Table 13 Satisfaction in ministry

	Yes %	? %	No %
I feel satisfied with my work in the church	73	16	11
I feel I am accomplishing things in my ministry	86	12	2
I am successful at overcoming difficulties within my ministry	62	34	4
I feel I am growing spiritually in my ministry	77	18	5
I have enough money to live comfortably	77	10	14

The survey results show that about three quarters of the women deacons (73%) felt satisfied with their work in the church, while 11% clearly felt dissatisfied and the remaining 16% felt neither satisfied nor dissatisfied. In one sense, these statistics reveal that there was a high level of job satisfaction experienced by women deacons. In another sense, however, the fact that 27% were not experiencing job satisfaction should be a matter of some concern, given both the nature of vocation to the clerical profession and the fact that at the time of the survey none of the women would have been ordained deacon for more than seven years.

The second fact revealed by the survey is that the majority of women deacons felt that they were accomplishing things in their ministry (86%) and that they were growing spiritually in their ministry (77%). Both of these statistics confirm that, in spite of difficulties and stresses, women deacons experienced a great deal of personal satisfaction and personal growth from their ministry.

Ministry is rarely without challenges and difficulties. Overall, the majority of the women deacons were much more inclined to feel that they were on top of their challenges and difficulties rather than that their challenges and difficulties were on top of them. Thus, 62% of the women deacons said that they were successful at overcoming difficulties within their ministry, compared with only 4% who said that they failed to overcome difficulties within their ministry. At the same time, however, the remaining 34% of the women deacons were none too confident that they always won against the difficulties.

Finally, the statistics demonstrate that the majority of the women deacons were content with their stipend. Three quarters (77%) said that they had enough money to live comfortably and another 10% refused to complain. This left, however, a significant minority of the women deacons, one in every seven (14%) who felt that they did *not* have enough money to live comfortably.

Does age make a difference?

Comparison between the four cohorts of women deacons (those under the age of forty, those in their forties, those in their fifties, and those aged sixty or over) reveals five interesting trends in the nature of satisfaction in ministry.

First, the proportion of women deacons who experienced personal accomplishment in their ministry remained constant across the four cohorts. Thus, 88% of the women deacons under the age of forty reported that they felt they were accomplishing things in their ministry, and so did 86% of the women deacons in the other three cohorts.

Second, the proportion of women deacons who felt that they coped with difficulties in their ministry remained constant across the four cohorts. Thus, 63% of the women deacons under the age of forty reported that they were successful at overcoming difficulties in their ministry, and so did 64% of the women deacons aged sixty or over.

Third, in spite of the consistent response to the items concerned with personal accomplishment and coping with difficulties, there was a slight drop in overall satisfaction with ministry across the four cohorts. While 77% of the women deacons aged under forty said that they felt satisfied with their work in the church, the proportion fell to 72% among those in their forties and fifties, and to 71% among the women deacons aged sixty or over.

Fourth, there was a general increase with age in the proportions of the women deacons who were aware of their own spiritual growth. Thus, the percentage of women deacons who reported that they were growing spiritually in their ministry grew from 68% among those under forty, to between 77% and 79% among those in their forties and fifties, and to 85% among those aged sixty or over.

Finally, there was a small increase with age in the proportions of women deacons who felt that they had enough money to live comfortably, from 75% among those aged under forty, to 76% among those in their forties, 77% among those in their fifties and 80% among those aged sixty or over.

Does marital status make a difference?

The levels of satisfaction in ministry experienced by the married women deacons and by the single women deacons were really quite similar. For example, 62% of the single women deacons reported that they were successful in overcoming difficulties in their ministry, and so did 64% of the married women deacons. Three quarters (76%) of the single women deacons felt that they were growing spiritually, and so did 77% of the married women deacons.

The profile of the widowed women deacons differed from the profile of the married women deacons in three important ways. The widowed women deacons were less likely than the married women deacons to have felt that they were successful at overcoming difficulties in their ministry (53% compared with 64%). The widowed women deacons were less likely than the married women deacons to have had enough money to live comfortably (71% compared with 77%). On the other hand, the widowed women deacons were more likely than the married women deacons to feel that they were growing spiritually in their ministry (85% compared with 77%).

The profile of the divorced women deacons differed from the profile of the married women deacons in two important ways. The divorced women deacons were more likely than the married women deacons to feel that they were accomplishing things in their ministry (93% compared with 85%). This may suggest that some divorced clergy compensate for possible failure in their personal lives by investing more heavily in their ministry role. The divorced women deacons were less likely than the married women deacons to feel that they had enough money to live comfortably (61% compared with 77%). This may suggest that some divorced clergy are suffering financially from marriage break-up.

Does church tradition make a difference?

There was very little difference in the level of satisfaction reported by women deacons who described themselves as Catholics and by women deacons who describe themselves as Evangelicals. Thus, 63% of the Evangelicals felt that they were successful in overcoming difficulties within their ministry, and so did 61% of the Catholics. Three quarters (76%) of the Evangelicals felt that they were growing spiritually and so did 76% of the Catholics. Three quarters (75%) of the Evangelicals felt satisfied with their work in the church and so did 73% of the Catholics. Three quarters (75%) of the Catholics felt that they had enough money to live comfortably, and so did 77% of the Evangelicals. On the other hand, the women deacons who described themselves as Evangelicals were more likely to say they felt they were accomplishing things in their ministry (89% compared with 85%).

The women deacons who described themselves as middle way Anglicans differed in no significant ways from the women deacons who described themselves as Catholics in respect of satisfaction in ministry.

Are non-stipendiaries different?

It is sometimes argued that non-stipendiary ministry fails to bring the same sense of satisfaction as afforded by stipendiary ministry, and that this accounts, at least in part, for the desire of a number of non-stipendiary clergy to transfer into stipendiary ministry. The present data offer some support for this view.

While four our of every five (79%) women deacons engaged in stipendiary ministry claimed that they felt satisfied with their work in the church, the proportion fell to 64% among non-stipendiary women deacons. While two out of every three (66%) women deacons engaged in stipendiary ministry claimed that they were successful at overcoming difficulties in their ministry, the proportion fell to 53% among non-stipendiary women deacons. While 89% of the women deacons engaged in stipendiary ministry felt that they were accomplishing things in their ministry, the proportion fell to 84% among non-stipendiary women deacons.

In spite of these clear differences in levels of satisfaction over several areas of ministry, roughly equal proportions of stipendiary women deacons and non-stipendiary women deacons felt that they were growing spiritually in their ministry.

There may be considerable variation in the economic resources of non-stipendiary women deacons. Some may be in well paid secular employment, some in less well paid secular employment, some unwaged married women, and others unwaged single women. Overall, the present data suggest that the non-stipendiary women deacons may feel somewhat less well off than the stipendiary women deacons. While four out of every five (81%) of the stipendiary women deacons felt that they had enough money to live comfortably, the proportion fell to 71% among the non-stipendiary women deacons.

Hearing the stories

It is clear from the personal stories told by the women deacons that many of them derived a strong sense of satisfaction with their ministry from three main areas.

First, for some women deacons this source of satisfaction came through a feeling of accomplishment when rising to meet the challenges of their ministry.

> I enjoy the ministry enormously, high satisfaction working in the inner city, and especially having responsibility for a church of my own. *(stipendiary, Deacon in charge aged 42)*

Second, other women deacons clearly derived satisfaction from overcoming difficulties within their ministry.

> I certainly cannot complain about being given too little responsibility or scope. My problems are trying to manage a demanding diocesan job and run a busy community church, but on balance I am one of the lucky ones. *(stipendiary, Deacon in Charge aged 59)*

In such situations, however, it remained important to keep a sense of perspective. As one woman deacon noted, it was because she was given lots of opportunities that it was sometimes necessary to stop to think things through.

> I felt very affirmed in ministry and almost given too many opportunities. Hence the need to stop and think and do some study because there was not enough time in a parish ministry. *(stipendiary, deacon on sabbatical aged 44)*

Third, growth and development in ministry were clearly important in order to maintain the feeling of satisfaction. For this woman deacon it was clear that this went hand in hand with a sense of answering God's call to ministry.

> I have found my experience of ministry personally and professionally very satisfying. I feel very strongly I am where God wants me to be. *(non-stipendiary, parish deacon aged 50)*

However, for some women deacons the sense of satisfaction could be quite tenuous when the situation in which they have been placed to minister changed. For one woman such change occurred on the arrival of a new curate who clearly upset the balance that had previously existed among those ministering in the parish.

> Satisfaction disappeared at appointment of new assistant curate. *(non-stipendiary, parish deacon aged 64)*

Fourth, listening to those women deacons who were part of a clergy couple, it became clear that many were expected to be non-stipendiary, while their husband served in a stipendiary role. In some cases this put a financial burden on the family which led to dissatisfaction with ministry. This situation also left women deacons feeling undervalued by the church. One woman deacon made the point in the following way.

> I actually would love to be fulltime to work in partnership with my husband and even to be paid enough to make full-time ministry possible. The situation is very hard. *(non-stipendiary, assistant curate aged 43)*

It is clear that for some dioceses a rethink of diocesan policy would have been most helpful to the women deacons, as one woman deacon pointed out.

> I am currently not eligible for stipendiary work as my diocese's policy is that only one stipend may be paid to a household. *(non-stipendiary, assistant curate aged 32)*

14 Public role

Introduction

One important part of the clerical profession concerns all those functions which demand an extraverting or public role. These functions include visiting people in their homes, visiting people in hospital, acting as teachers, working as evangelists, or becoming leaders in the local community.

Some of these functions may need a high level of interpersonal skill and empathy. Others of these functions may need the ability to stand out in the crowd or to take a public lead. Public roles such as these may be carried out differently by male clergy and women deacons. Some people, for example, might argue that women deacons would see themselves as having particular skills to offer in areas like hospital visiting and consequently make a better job of this aspect of ministry than male clergy. Conversely women deacons might see themselves as less well equipped for areas like becoming leaders in the local community and consequently make a less satisfactory job of this aspect of ministry than male clergy. Other people, however, might reject such stereotypes as totally inappropriate and inaccurate.

This chapter sets out, therefore, to ascertain whether women deacons considered themselves to be better than male clergy in certain public areas of ministry. The specific public roles selected for analysis are the clergy as visitors, hospital visitors, teachers, evangelists, and leaders in the local community.

Overview

The survey results show that the majority of women deacons were reticent about making claims that women clergy tend to be better than male clergy in areas concerned with the public role of ministry. On average, half the women deacons (51%) disagreed with the five items in this section and a further 37% preferred the 'not certain' response. This means that, on average, only 12% of the women deacons agreed with the five items in this section.

Table 14 Public role

	Yes %	? %	No %
Women clergy tend to be better:			
visitors than male clergy	27	28	45
hospital visitors than male clergy	21	36	43
teachers than male clergy	9	38	53
leaders in the local community than male clergy	3	41	56
evangelists than male clergy	2	42	57

The statistics also demonstrate that, when the women deacons considered women clergy to be better than male clergy in any of these public roles of ministry, they were likely to highlight the role of visitor. Thus one in four (27%) of the women deacons agreed that women clergy tend to be better visitors than male clergy, and one in five (21%) of the women deacons agreed that women clergy tend to be better hospital visitors than male clergy.

Like the role of visitor, the role of teaching, too, is sometimes seen as an area in which women clergy may excel. Just 9% of the women deacons, however, agreed that women clergy tend to be better teachers than male clergy. The proportions then fell even further to 3% of women deacons who agreed that women clergy tend to make better leaders in the local community than male clergy and to 2% of women deacons who agreed that women clergy make better evangelists than male clergy.

Overall these statistics confirm the stereotype that women deacons saw themselves making better visitors than public leaders.

Does age make a difference?

Agreement with the stereotype that women clergy make better visitors than male clergy was very clearly age-related. The younger women deacons were much less likely to endorse this stereotype than the older women deacons. For example, while 45% of the women deacons aged sixty or over agreed that women clergy tend to be better visitors than male clergy, the proportions fell to 30% among the women deacons in their fifties, to 22% among the women deacons in their forties, and to 15% among the women deacons aged under forty. While 36% of the women deacons aged sixty or over agreed that women clergy tend to be better hospital visitors than male clergy, the proportions fell to 25% among the women deacons in their fifties, to 15% among the women deacons in their forties, and to 13% among the women deacons aged under forty.

Agreement with the stereotype that women clergy make better teachers than male clergy was also clearly age-related. While 16% of the women deacons aged sixty or over agreed that women clergy tend to be better teachers than male clergy, the proportions fell to 11% among the women deacons in their fifties, to 7% among the women deacons in their forties, and to 4% among the women deacons aged under forty.

There were no age related trends regarding the minority of women deacons who considered that women clergy tend to be better evangelists or better leaders in the local community than male clergy.

Does marital status make a difference?

Single women deacons were more likely than married women deacons to have supported the view that women clergy make better visitors than male clergy. For example, while a quarter (24%) of the married women deacons felt that women clergy tend to be better visitors than male clergy, the proportion rose to 30% among the single women deacons. While 18% of the married women deacons felt that women clergy tend to be better hospital visitors than male clergy, the proportion rose to 26% among the single women deacons.

On the other hand, the single women deacons and married women deacons did not differ in their views on women clergy as teachers, leaders in the local community or evangelists.

The views of the widowed women deacons closely followed those of the single women deacons, while the views of the divorced women deacons clearly followed those of the married women deacons.

Does church tradition make a difference?

Women deacons across the three church traditions (Catholic, middle way, and Evangelical) held similar views on women clergy as visitors. Thus, 25% of the Catholics, 26% of the middle way Anglicans, and 28% of the Evangelicals considered that women clergy tend to be better visitors than male clergy. Similarly, 22% of the Catholics, 23% of the middle way Anglicans, and 20% of the Evangelicals considered that women clergy tend to be better hospital visitors than male clergy.

The only significant difference according to church tradition within this set of items concerned the role of clergy as teacher. Evangelicals were less inclined to accept the view that women clergy are better teachers. Thus, only 6% of the women deacons who described themselves as Evangelicals supported the view that women clergy tend to be better teachers than male clergy, compared with 12% of the women deacons who described themselves as Catholics and 11% of the women deacons who described themselves as middle way Anglicans.

Are non-stipendiaries different?

The attitudes of the stipendiary women deacons and the non-stipendiary women deacons toward the comparative contribution of male and female clergy to public ministry roles are very similar. This point is illustrated by the following statistics.

Of the stipendiary women deacons, 26% considered that women clergy tend to be better visitors than male clergy, and so did 28% of the non-stipendiary women deacons. Less than one in ten (8%) of the stipendiary women deacons considered that women clergy tend to be better teachers than male clergy, and so did 7% of the non-stipendiary women deacons. Only 3% of the stipendiary women deacons considered that women clergy tend to be better leaders in the local community than male clergy, and so did 2% of the non-stipendiary women deacons. Only 2% of the stipendiary women deacons considered that women clergy tend to be better evangelists than male clergy, and so did 2% of the non-stipendiary women deacons.

Hearing the stories

Listening to the personal stories told by the women deacons, four main issues emerge relating to the public role of their ministry.

First, for many women deacons the local secular community was an important forum for their public role, as well as the local Christian community. For one woman deacon the relationship between the two communities was clearly viewed in a reciprocal way.

> I also see the Christian community as having something to say and learn from the local community. *(stipendiary, sector minister aged 55)*

Another woman deacon reported how important acceptance by the local secular community was for her.

> The community's acceptance of me was vital. *(stipendiary, parish deacon aged 52)*

Second, for some women deacons, visiting their parishioners was an important part of the public role of this ministry in the community.

> I work in a rural area, therefore, visiting people in the community, social events etc. have a very high priority and it is possible to visit most parishioners in hospital. *(stipendiary, parish deacon aged 44)*

However, for others in urban areas visiting has to be more selective as the density of the population allows.

Third, listening to the women deacons it is clear that many considered evangelism to be in the form of the example they give. For some, who held secular employment along with a parish position, the opportunity is perhaps greater.

> I see my job as a teacher as part of my ministry. Taking the church into a secular institution - ministry to pupils and colleagues. *(non-stipendiary, parish deacon aged 55)*

Fourth, some of the women deacons found that they suffered by having their personal lives put under scrutiny while their public role was largely ignored.

> I suspect you will find in general low expectations of women on their public ministry, and high expectations set on their personal lives. *(stipendiary, cathedral clergy aged 36)*

It is clear from these accounts that for some women deacons the public role could bring unwanted scrutiny, while for others a role within the community was a vital and visible part of their ministry.

15 Pastoral role

Introduction

A second important part of the clerical profession concerns all those functions which demand a more introverting or pastoral role. For example, clergy may find themselves working with young couples in marriage preparation, or in preparing them for the baptism of their babies. Clergy may find themselves preparing small groups of teenagers or adults for confirmation.

On some occasions clergy may find themselves working with couples at times of marriage breakdown or crises. At other times they need to stand alongside the bereaved and become involved with bereavement counselling. Then people may turn to the clergy for spiritual direction.

All of these pastoral roles may be carried out differently by male clergy and women deacons. This chapter sets out to ascertain whether women deacons considered themselves to be better than male clergy in such pastoral areas of ministry. The specific pastoral roles selected for analysis are baptism preparation, confirmation preparation, marriage preparation, marital counselling, bereavement counselling and spiritual direction.

Overview

The survey results show that, just as the majority of women deacons were reticent about making claims that women clergy tend to be better than male clergy in areas concerned with the public role of ministry, so they are reluctant to make claims that women clergy tend to be better than male clergy in areas concerned with the pastoral role of ministry. On average almost half the women deacons (48%) disagree with the six items in this section and a further 37% preferred the 'not certain' response. This means that, on average, only 15% of the women deacons agreed with the six items in this section.

Table 15 Pastoral role

	Yes %	? %	No %
Women clergy tend to be better:			
at baptism preparation than male clergy	16	35	48
at confirmation preparation than male clergy	6	42	52
at marriage preparation than male clergy	13	39	48
at marital counselling than male clergy	15	38	47
at bereavement counselling than male clergy	30	26	45
spiritual directors than male clergy	13	39	48

Of the six pastoral roles listed in this section, the area in which the women deacons were most likely to think that women clergy excelled over male clergy was bereavement counselling. This view was expressed by three women deacons in every ten (30%).

Between one in six and one in eight of the women deacons considered that women clergy were better than male clergy at baptism preparation (16%), marital counselling (15%), marriage preparation (13%) and spiritual direction (13%). The proportion fell to one in seventeen of the women deacons (6%) who considered that women clergy tend to be better at confirmation preparation than male clergy.

Overall these statistics confirm the stereotype that women deacons saw themselves as particularly sensitive to the needs of those who are most vulnerable, like the bereaved.

Does age make a difference?

Agreement with the stereotype that women clergy make better pastors than male clergy is clearly age related. Younger women deacons were less likely to endorse this stereotype than older women deacons. This point is illustrated by the statistics comparing the view of the women deacons across the four cohorts (those under the age of forty, those in their forties, those in their fifties, and those aged sixty or over).

While nearly half (46%) of the women deacons aged sixty or over considered that women clergy tended to be better at bereavement counselling than male clergy, the proportions fell to a third (32%) of the women deacons in their fifties, to a quarter (24%) of the women deacons in their forties, and to a fifth (21%) of the women deacons aged under forty.

While 29% of the women deacons aged sixty or over considered that women clergy tended to be better at baptism preparation than male clergy, the proportions fell to 18% among the women deacons in their fifties, to 13% among the women deacons in their forties, and to 9% among the women deacons aged under forty.

While 23% of the women deacons aged sixty or over considered that women deacons tended to be better at marriage preparation than male clergy, the proportions fell to 15% among the women deacons in their fifties, to 10% among the women deacons in their forties, and to 8% among the women deacons aged under forty.

While 20% of the women deacons aged sixty or over considered that women clergy tended to be better at marital counselling than male clergy, the proportions fell to 18% among the women deacons in their fifties, to 14% among the women deacons in their forties, and to 9% among the women deacons aged under forty.

While 19% of the women deacons aged sixty or over considered that women clergy tended to be better spiritual directors than male clergy, the proportions fell to 13% among the women deacons in their fifties, to 11% among the women deacons in their forties, and to 9% among the women deacons aged under forty.

The consistent way in which the ministry gender stereotypes espoused by the older women deacons are being progressively eroded among their younger colleagues is consistent with the ways in which gender stereotypes as a whole have been increasingly questioned and overturned by successive generations of women.

Does marital status make a difference?

While the previous chapter identified little by way of difference between the single women deacons and the married women deacons in their perceptions of the public ministry of women, greater differences emerged in the present chapter in their perceptions of the pastoral ministry of women. These differences are specifically in relation to their views concerning marriage preparation, marriage counselling and bereavement counselling.

First, the married women deacons were more inclined than the single women deacons to maintain that women clergy are better than male clergy at marriage preparation. Thus, 14% of the married women deacons felt that women clergy tend to be better at marriage preparation than male clergy, compared with 10% of the single women deacons.

Second, the married women deacons were more inclined than the single women deacons to maintain that women clergy were better than male clergy at marital counselling. Thus, 17% of the married women deacons felt that women clergy tend to be better at marital counselling than male clergy, compared with 10% of the single women deacons.

Third, in the area of bereavement counselling, it is the single women deacons who were more inclined than the married women deacons to maintain that women clergy are better than male clergy. Thus, 36% of the single women deacons felt that women clergy tend to be better at bereavement counselling than male clergy, compared with 26% of the married women deacons.

The profile of the widowed women deacons differed from that of the married women deacons only in respect of one area of the pastoral roles of ministry, namely bereavement counselling. While 26% of the married women deacons considered that women clergy are better at bereavement counselling than male clergy, the proportion rose to 32% among the widowed women deacons. In this case the judgement may be influenced by personal experience.

Overall, the divorced women deacons displayed a little greater confidence in the superiority of the pastoral ministry of women, compared with the married women deacons. This point is illustrated by the following statistics.

While 11% of the married women deacons maintained that women clergy tend to be better spiritual directors than male clergy, the proportion rose to 20% among the divorced women deacons. While 26% of the married women deacons maintained that women clergy tend to be better at bereavement counselling than male clergy, the proportion rose to 30% among the divorced women deacons. While 14% of the married women deacons maintained that women clergy tend to be better at marriage preparation than male clergy, the proportion rose to 18% among the divorced women deacons.

Does church tradition make a difference?

Overall, women deacons who identified with the Evangelical wing of the Anglican church tended to display a little less confidence in the superiority of the pastoral ministry of women, compared with women deacons who identified with the Catholic wing of the Anglican church. This point is illustrated by the following statistics.

While 18% of the Catholic women deacons maintained that women clergy tend to be better at baptism preparation than male clergy, the proportion fell a little to 14% among the Evangelical women deacons. While 17% of the Catholic women deacons maintained that women clergy tend to be better at marital counselling than male clergy, the proportion fell a little to 13% among the Evangelical women deacons. While 16% of the Catholic women deacons maintained that women clergy tend to be better at marriage preparation than male clergy, the proportion fell a little to 11% among the Evangelical women deacons. While 15% of the Catholic women deacons maintained that women clergy tend to be better spiritual directors than male clergy, the proportion fell a little to 10% among the Evangelical women deacons. While 8% of the Catholic women deacons maintained that women clergy tend to be better at confirmation preparation than male clergy, the proportion fell a little to 4% among the Evangelical women deacons.

The profile of the women deacons who identified with middle way Anglicanism followed a similar pattern to the profile of the women deacons who identified with the Catholic wing of the Anglican church.

Are non-stipendiaries different?

There were no significant differences between the attitudes of the stipendiary women deacons and the non-stipendiary women deacons in respect of the superiority of the pastoral ministry of women clergy in the three areas of confirmation preparation, spiritual direction, and bereavement counselling. While 5% of the stipendiary women deacons maintained that women clergy tend to be better at confirmation preparation than male clergy, so did 6% of the non-stipendiary women deacons. While 12% of the stipendiary women deacons maintained that women clergy tend to be better spiritual directors than male clergy, so did 10% of the non-stipendiary women deacons. While 29% of the stipendiary women deacons maintained that women clergy tend to be better at bereavement counselling than male clergy, so did 31% of the non-stipendiary women deacons.

On the other hand, the non-stipendiary women deacons displayed a little greater confidence in the superiority of the pastoral ministry of women clergy in respect of the three areas of baptism preparation, marriage preparation and marital counselling. While 14% of the stipendiary women deacons maintained that women clergy tend to be better at baptism preparation than male clergy, the proportion rose a little among the non-stipendiary women deacons to 19%. While 12% of the stipendiary women deacons maintained that women clergy tend to be better at marital counselling than male clergy, the proportion rose a little among the non-stipendiary women deacons to 18%. While 11% of the stipendiary women deacons maintained that women clergy tend to be better at marriage preparation than male clergy, the proportion rose a little among the non-stipendiary women deacons to 15%.

Hearing the stories

The personal stories told by the women deacons in respect of their pastoral role demonstrate a wide diversity in their ministry. As well as working in the traditional areas of ministry, these stories demonstrate how women deacons have been led into new areas of pastoral ministry.

First, a number of women deacons reported how the feedback from funeral services they have conducted has been very positive. Some of the women deacons have gone on to relate how the bereaved have found women particularly helpful in counselling.

> Funerals and bereavement counselling - in this area people have said that female clergy are better. *(non-stipendiary, parish deacon aged 38)*

Second, some women found that clerical dress acted as a bridge, making them more approachable to people and more available for pastoral ministry. In clerical dress they felt they were perceived as available to help others.

> I wear a collar to enable parishioners to easily identify me, and know that I am at work, therefore improving approachability. *(stipendiary, parish deacon aged 42)*

Third, some women deacons found that their pastoral role had become shaped by specific experiences or influenced by the specific needs of some individuals to whom they had ministered.

> I have become deeply involved in the AIDS issue as a result of one parishioner. *(non-stipendiary, assistant curate aged 36)*

Finally, some women deacons felt it was both necessary and important to draw a distinction between their pastoral role as a spiritual director and the role of counsellor. They recognised that some people needed the skilled help of a professional counsellor and thought that they were not themselves qualified to offer such help. In this way they showed a proper recognition of their own professional limitations. This following woman deacon is an example of that response.

> Apart from spiritual direction, only qualified counsellors should deal with real counselling. *(stipendiary, parish deacon aged 47)*

These accounts demonstrate a strong commitment by the women deacons to a pastoral role within their ministry. These accounts also demonstrate a recognition that sometimes women deacons were felt by their parishioners to handle situations more effectively than their male colleagues.

> Many people have said to me that they have had better experiences with female clergy - my answers reflect these comments. *(stipendiary, parish deacon aged 37)*

16 Social role

Introduction

A third important part of the clerical profession concerns all those functions which constitute the social role of the clergy. For example, there are expectations that clergy should be competent to work among different age categories of young people. Many churches operate parent and toddler groups or play groups which expect clergy to work successfully among pre-schoolers. Many churches promote contacts with local primary schools, either because these schools are voluntary aided, voluntary controlled, or grant maintained church foundations, or because county schools welcome links with the wider community. Such contacts expect clergy to work successfully among primary school children. Many churches also expect clergy to work successfully among teenagers, either by visiting local secondary schools or through youth groups.

Many churches also run regular groups for women. A small number of churches run similar groups for men. Often the clergy are expected to contribute to such groups and to work successfully in groups which may have only women as members or only men as members.

Once again, all these social roles may be carried out differently by male clergy and by women clergy. This chapter sets out to ascertain whether women deacons considered themselves to be better than male clergy in such social roles of ministry. The specific social roles selected for analysis are work with pre-school children, work with primary school children, work with teenagers, work with men's groups and work with women's groups.

Overview

The survey results show that, just as the majority of the women deacons were reticent about claiming women clergy to be better than male clergy in areas concerned with the public or pastoral roles of ministry, so they are reluctant to make claims that women clergy tend to be better than male clergy in areas concerned with the social role of ministry. On average half the women deacons (49%) disagreed with the five items in this section and a further 33% preferred the 'not certain' response. This means that, on average, only 18% of the women deacons agreed with the five items in this section.

Table 16 Social role

	Yes %	? %	No %
Women clergy tend to be better at work with:			
pre-school children than male clergy	31	27	42
primary school children than male clergy	18	34	48
teenagers than male clergy	3	41	56
men's groups than male clergy	2	37	61
women's groups than male clergy	36	26	38

Of the five social roles listed, the two areas in which the women deacons were most likely to think that women clergy excelled over male clergy were work with women's groups and work with pre-school children. Thus, 36% of the women deacons agreed that clergy women tend to be better at work with women's groups than male clergy. Similarly, 31% of the women deacons agreed that women clergy tend to be better at work with pre-school children than male clergy.

At the same time, nearly one in five (18%) of the women deacons agreed that women clergy tend to be better at work with primary school children than male clergy. On the other hand, very few women deacons promoted the view that women clergy were better than male clergy at work with teenagers (3%) or with men's groups (2%).

These statistics confirm the stereotype that women deacons saw themselves working best with young children and women.

Does age make a difference?

Close analysis of the relationship between age and the women deacons' perceptions of the social aspects of ministry reveals three main trends.

First, agreement with the stereotype that women clergy are better than male clergy at ministry with pre-school children and with primary school children was very clearly age related. The younger women deacons were less likely to endorse this stereotype than the older women deacons. While nearly half (46%) of the women deacons aged sixty or over considered that women clergy tend to be better at work with pre-school children than male clergy, the proportions fell to around a third (35%) of the women deacons in their fifties, to a little over a quarter (28%) of the women deacons in their forties, and to less than a fifth (18%) of the women deacons aged under forty. While 28% of the women deacons aged sixty or over considered that women clergy tend to be better at work with primary school children than male clergy, the proportions fell to 19% among the women deacons in their fifties, to 15% among the women deacons in their forties, and to 13% among the women deacons aged under forty.

Second, agreement with the stereotype that women clergy are better at work with women's groups shows a less linear trend with age. While 45% of the women deacons aged sixty or over considered that women clergy tend to be better at work with women's groups than male clergy, the proportion fell to 33% among the women deacons in their fifties, and then the proportions remained fairly constant at 36% among women deacons in their forties and 34% among women deacons aged under forty.

Third, the small percentage of women deacons who considered that women clergy are better than male clergy at work with teenagers (3%) or with men's groups (2%) does not fluctuate significantly across the four age cohorts.

Does marital status make a difference?

The perceptions of the single women deacons and the married women deacons agreed quite closely in respect of four of the five social roles listed in the survey. Thus, 38% of the single women deacons agreed that women clergy tend to be better at work with women's groups than male clergy, and so did 35% of the married women deacons. A third (33%) of the single women deacons agreed that women clergy tend to be better at work with pre-school children than male clergy, and so did 30% of the married women deacons. Only between 2% and 3% of the single women deacons and the married women deacons agreed that women clergy tend to be better than male clergy at work with teenagers or with men's groups.

On the other hand, the perceptions of the single women deacons and the married women deacons agreed less closely when it came to considering work with primary school children. While 22% of the single women deacons considered that women clergy tend to be better at work with primary school children than male clergy, the proportion dropped to 15% among the married women deacons. Possibly closer familiarity with children in this age range had done something to change the perceptions of some of the married women deacons.

The profile of the widowed women deacons followed that of the married women deacons regarding their perceptions of the social role of women in ministry, except in relationship to their perception of work with women's groups. While 35% of the married women deacons considered that women clergy tend to be better at work with women's groups than male clergy, the proportion dropped to 31% among the widowed women deacons.

The profile of the divorced women deacons followed that of the single women deacons rather than that of the married women deacons in this chapter.

Does church tradition make a difference?

The perceptions of the social role of women in ministry held by the women deacons who described themselves as on the Catholic wing of the church differed from the perceptions of the women deacons who described themselves as on the Evangelical wing of the church in two ways.

First, the women deacons on the Evangelical wing of the church were more inclined to emphasise the distinctive contribution which women clergy make to ministry among children. Thus, 36% of the Evangelical women deacons considered that women clergy tend to be better at work with pre-school children than male clergy, compared with 27% of the Catholic women deacons. Similarly, 20% of the Evangelical women deacons considered that women clergy tend to be better at work with primary school children than male clergy, compared with 15% of the Catholic women deacons.

Second, the women deacons on the Evangelical wing of the church were also more inclined to emphasise the distinctive contribution which women clergy make to ministry among women's groups. Thus, 40% of the Evangelical women deacons considered that women clergy tend to be better at work with women's groups than male clergy, compared with 33% of the Catholic women deacons.

The women deacons who described themselves as middle way Anglicans generally followed the same profile as the Evangelical women deacons, except in two respects. The middle way Anglican women deacons were less inclined than the Evangelical women deacons to support the view that women clergy are better than male clergy at work with pre-school children (30% compared with 36%). The middle way Anglican women deacons were also less inclined than the Evangelical women deacons to support the view that women clergy are better at work with women's groups than male clergy (35% compared with 40%).

Are non-stipendiaries different?

In most respects the perceptions of non-stipendiary women deacons regarding the social role of women in ministry were similar to the perceptions of the stipendiary women deacons. For example, 18% of the non-stipendiary women deacons considered that women clergy tend to be better at work with primary school children than male clergy, and so did 18% of the stipendiary women deacons. Just 2% of the non-stipendiary women deacons considered that women clergy tend to be better at work with teenagers than male clergy, and so did 2% of the stipendiary women deacons.

On the other hand, there is a significant difference between the perceptions of the non-stipendiary women deacons and the perceptions of the stipendiary women deacons regarding the superiority of women clergy's work among pre-school children. While over one quarter (28%) of the stipendiary women deacons considered that women clergy tend to be better at work with pre-school children than male clergy, the proportion rose to over one third (36%) of the non-stipendiary women deacons.

Hearing the stories

On listening to the personal stories of the women deacons concerning their social roles in ministry three points are clear.

First, a number of the women deacons recognised that it was not necessarily because they were better at work with children that some parishioners preferred women clergy rather than male clergy doing this work. Rather people in their parish simply tended to feel more comfortable with a woman working with young children, as this woman deacon says.

> People generally are more comfortable with women working with toddlers, so I think women find it easier to gain access to them than their male colleagues. *(stipendiary, assistant curate aged 32)*

Second, many of the women deacons expressed the view that the ability to work with children was not dependent on gender. The following woman deacon's response is a typical illustration of this point.

> I think gender matters very little in work with children. Either you have the gift to work with children or you do not. *(stipendiary, parish deacon aged 46)*

Third, on turning attention to the issue of working with adults, there is a mixed response to the usefulness of men's groups and women's groups. One point of view is expressed by the following woman deacon.

> I find the women's group in our parish useful. The women are a lot more forthcoming than they would be in a mixed group. *(non-stipendiary, parish deacon aged 51)*

There are other women deacons who do not think such division into separate groups for men and women is helpful. This alternative perspective was voiced by the woman deacon who said.

> I find single sex groups artificial. *(stipendiary, deacon in charge aged 43)*

It is clear from the comments of these women deacons that the church cannot assume that clergy women are going to consider themselves to be better at certain roles than their male counterparts simply because of their gender. The message clearly is that individual clergy, both male and female, need to be assessed according to their individual gifts.

17 Liturgical role

Introduction

A fourth important part of the clerical profession concerns the liturgical functions of the clergy. Many of these liturgical functions can be performed equally by deacons and by priests. Both may lead public worship and conduct the statutory services of matins and evensong. Both may preach. Both may be involved in the occasional offices of baptisms, weddings and funerals.

The ordination of women to the diaconate, therefore, opened these liturgical roles to women. At the same time, however, the restrictions placed on the office of deacon, in comparison with the office of priest, imposed subtle differences in the way in which the liturgical roles of ministry could be fulfilled and expressed by women deacons and by male priests. Clergy in deacons' orders remain unable to pronounce absolution and blessing. At these places in the services deacons are obliged to use a different form of wording from that prescribed for priests.

Once again these liturgical roles may be carried out differently by male clergy and women clergy. This chapter sets out to ascertain whether women deacons considered themselves to be better than male clergy in such liturgical roles of ministry. The specific liturgical roles selected for analysis are leadership of public worship, preaching, conducting baptisms, conducting marriages, and conducting funerals.

Overview

The survey results show that the majority of the women deacons were reluctant to make claims that women clergy tend to be better than male clergy in the liturgical roles of ministry, just as they were reticent about making such claims *vis à vis* the public, pastoral or social roles. On average over half the women deacons (51%) disagreed with the five items in this section and a further 36% preferred the 'not certain' response. This means that, on average, only 13% of the women deacons agreed with the five items in this section.

Table 17 Liturgical role

	Yes %	? %	No %
Women clergy tend to be better:			
at conducting baptisms than male clergy	14	36	50
at conducting marriage than male clergy	12	37	51
at conducting funerals than male clergy	27	28	45
preachers than male clergy	5	39	56
leaders of public worship than male clergy	8	38	55

Of the five liturgical roles listed, the one area in which the women deacons were most likely to think that women clergy excelled over male clergy was conducting funerals. This view was espoused by over a quarter of the women deacons (27%). A significant minority of the women deacons also maintained that women clergy tend to be better than male clergy at conducting baptisms (14%) and conducting marriages (12%). These three liturgical functions (funerals, baptisms and weddings) are all experiences of the pastoral ministry of the church shaped to the needs of specific individuals.

On the other hand, there is less commitment to the view that women clergy are better than male clergy at conducting the public offices of the church. The proportion dropped to 8% of the women deacons who considered that women clergy are better at leading public worship than male clergy and to 5% of the women deacons who considered that women clergy are better preachers than male clergy.

Overall, these statistics confirm the stereotype that women deacons saw themselves as particularly well suited to dealing with the suffering of death and bereavement.

Does age make a difference?

Close analysis of the relationship between age and the women deacons' perceptions of the liturgical aspects of ministry reveals three main trends.

First, agreement with the stereotype that the women clergy are better than male clergy at conducting funerals was very clearly age related. The younger women deacons were less likely to endorse this stereotype than the older women deacons. While more than a third (36%) of the women deacons aged sixty or over considered that women clergy tend to be better at conducting funerals than male clergy, the proportions fell to 30% of the women deacons in their fifties, to 23% of the women deacons in their forties, and to 18% of the women deacons aged under forty.

Second, agreement with the view that women clergy are better than male clergy at conducting baptisms and marriages was also age related. Once again the younger women deacons were less likely to endorse these views than the older women deacons. While 23% of the women deacons aged sixty or over considered that women clergy tend to be better at conducting baptisms than male clergy, the proportions fell to 16% of the women deacons in their fifties, to 11% of the women deacons in their forties and to 9% of the women deacons aged under forty. While 16% of the women deacons aged sixty or over considered that women clergy tend to be better at conducting marriages than male clergy, the proportions fell to 14% of the women deacons in their forties, to 10% of the women deacons in their fifties, and to 9% of the women deacons aged under forty.

Third, while these views on the contribution of women clergy to the pastoral offices (funerals, baptisms and weddings) were clearly age-related, the same did not apply to views on the contribution of women clergy to the public offices of the church. The difference is reflected in two ways. To begin with, even among the oldest cohort less than one in ten women deacons considered that women clergy tend to be better than male clergy at leading public worship (8%) or at preaching (9%). This compares with the way in which large proportions of the women deacons aged sixty or over considered that women clergy tend to be better than male clergy at conducting funerals (36%), conducting baptisms (23%) and conducting marriages (16%). This attitude toward the contribution of women clergy to the public offices of the church remained more static across the age cohorts. While 8% of the women deacons aged sixty or over considered that women clergy tend to be better leaders of public worship than male clergy, the same view is held by 7% of the women deacons in their forties, and by 6% of the women deacons aged under forty. While 9% of the women deacons aged sixty or over considered that women clergy tend to be better preachers than male clergy, this same view is held by 6% of the women deacons in their forties.

Does marital status make a difference?

The perceptions of the single women deacons and the married women deacons agreed quite closely in respect of three of the five liturgical roles listed in the survey. Thus, 16% of the single women deacons considered that women clergy tend to be better at conducting baptisms than male clergy, and so did 14% of the married women deacons. One in twenty (5%) of the single women deacons considered that women clergy tend to be better preachers than male clergy, and so did 6% of the married women deacons.

Similarly, 9% of the single women deacons considered that women clergy tend to be better leaders of public worship than male clergy, and so did 7% of the married women deacons. There are, however, significant differences in the attitudes of the married women deacons and the single women deacons toward the contribution of women clergy in marriages and funerals.

On the one hand, married women deacons were more likely than single women deacons to emphasise the distinctive contribution of women clergy to weddings. Thus, 13% of the married women deacons maintained that women clergy tend to be better at conducting marriages than male clergy, compared with 9% of the single women deacons.

On the other hand, single women deacons were more likely than married women deacons to emphasise the distinctive contribution of women clergy to funerals. Thus, 32% of the single women deacons maintained that women clergy tend to be better at conducting funerals than male clergy, compared with 23% of the married women deacons.

The profile of the widowed women deacons followed that of the married women deacons regarding their perceptions of the liturgical role of women in ministry, except in relationship to their perception of conducting marriages. While 13% of the married women deacons considered that women clergy tend to be better at conducting marriages than male clergy, the proportion rose to 17% among the widowed women deacons.

The profile of the divorced women deacons did not significantly depart from the profile of the married women deacons in this chapter.

Does church tradition make a difference?

The perceptions of the liturgical role of women in ministry held by the women deacons who described themselves as Evangelicals differed from the perspectives of the women deacons who described themselves as Catholic in respect of just two of the five areas listed in this section of the survey. Evangelical women deacons were a little less likely than Catholic women deacons to maintain the superiority of women clergy at conducting marriages or at preaching. While 14% of the Catholic women deacons considered that women clergy are better at conducting marriages than male clergy, the proportion fell a little to 10% among the Evangelical women deacons.

While 8% of the Catholic women deacons considered that women clergy are better at preaching than male clergy, the proportion fell a little to 3% among the Evangelical women deacons.

On the other hand, there were no significant differences between the proportions of Catholic women deacons and Evangelical women deacons who considered that women clergy were better than male clergy at conducting baptisms (15% and 13%), at conducting funerals (26% and 28%), or at leading public worship (9% and 8%).

The women deacons who described themselves as middle way Anglicans generally followed the same profile as the Evangelical women deacons in their attitude toward the liturgical role of women in ministry.

Are non-stipendiaries different?

There are no significant differences between the proportions of non-stipendiary women deacons and stipendiary women deacons regarding the liturgical role of women in ministry. For example, 13% of the non-stipendiary women deacons considered that women clergy tend to be better at conducting baptisms than male clergy, and so did 13% of the stipendiary women deacons. Similarly 11% of the non-stipendiary women deacons considered that women clergy were better at conducting marriages than male clergy, and so did 12% of the stipendiary women deacons. One in four (25%) of the non-stipendiary women deacons considered that women clergy tend to be better at conducting funerals than male clergy, and so did 26% of the stipendiary women deacons.

Hearing the stories

On entering the diaconate women deacons were able to take on certain liturgical roles. However, listening to the personal stories of woman deacons concerning their liturgical role it is clear that this role was often restricted by those around them. Such restriction seems to have taken two main forms. First, restriction was imposed through discouragement, as illustrated by the following woman deacon.

> In this diocese deacons are not encouraged to marry or baptise. *(stipendiary, parish deacon aged 50)*

Second, restriction was imposed by making it clear that women deacons were only used as a 'last resort'. This point is illustrated by the following woman deacon.

> Weddings are not conducted by deacons in this diocese unless there is nobody else to do them. *(non-stipendiary, parish deacon aged 50)*

These kinds of restrictions meant that women deacons were not being given the chance to fully develop their liturgical role.

Despite such restrictions a number of women deacons reported positive feedback from those who attended services which they conducted. This woman's comment was typical of many.

> I get asked to conduct funerals, people seem more at ease with me in that situation. *(non-stipendiary, parish deacon aged 60)*

For other women deacons a separation between the non-sacramental aspects of liturgy and the sacramental aspects of liturgy brought a certain amount of freedom.

> There is total liturgical freedom, because two thirds of my ministry is mainly non-sacramental so the women priests issue does not influence what I can and cannot do. *(non-stipendiary, team minister aged 54)*

18 Inclusive language

Introduction

Masculine imagery and masculine language have been long engrained within the theology and liturgy of the Church of England. It came naturally to the culture of the 1662 *Book of Common Prayer* to address a mixed congregation of men and women with the invocation 'Dearly beloved brethren'. It apparently came equally naturally to the culture of the *Alternative Service Book 1980* to invite a mixed congregation to summarise their faith in the saving power of Christ with the phrase 'for us men and for our salvation'.

While male clergy within the Church of England appear to be becoming increasingly conscious of the embarrassment of sexist language, it may be anticipated that women deacons will be particularly aware of the incongruity between their own gender and the language frequently promoted in church services.

Against this background the present chapter has three main aims. The first aim of this chapter is to assess the attitude of the women deacons to the use of inclusive language. Specifically the issue is raised in relation to three different components of worship, namely service books, bible translations and hymns. Since the introduction of inclusive language into church services is likely to be a very controversial issue, the second aim of this chapter is to gauge the sensitivity of the women deacons to the likely controversy involved. The third aim of this chapter is to take one step beyond inclusive language to assess the views of the women deacons on the use of female imagery for God alongside the well established use of male imagery for God.

Overview

The survey results show that the majority of the women deacons were clearly in favour of the use of inclusive language within the church's liturgy. The strongest vote went for the use of inclusive language in service books, with somewhat lower commitment shown for the use of inclusive language in bible translations and in hymns. Thus, three quarters of the women deacons (75%) voted for the use of inclusive language in service books, and three fifths voted for the use of inclusive language in hymns (62%) and in bible translations (60%).

Table 18 Inclusive language

	Yes %	? %	No %
Inclusive language should be used in service books	75	16	9
Inclusive language should be used in bible translations	60	23	16
Inclusive language should be used in hymns	62	24	14
Use of inclusive language will be controversial in most congregations	47	28	25
Hymns and prayers should use female imagery for God	35	29	36

It is important to recognise that a significant minority of the women deacons stood out against the adoption of inclusive language in respect of bible translations (16%), hymns (14%) and service books (9%). While the majority of the women deacons were in favour of inclusive language, a number of them recognised that this would be controversial in most congregations. Half the women deacons (47%) considered that inclusive language would be controversial in most congregations, compared with a quarter (25%) who did not think that this would be the case.

The survey results also reveal that a much lower proportion of the women deacons supported the use of female imagery for God in hymns and prayers than supported the use of inclusive language in other areas. In fact the women deacons were divided into three almost equal groups on the use of female imagery for God. A little over one third supported the idea (35%) and a little over one third rejected the idea (36%), with the remaining third being undecided (29%).

Does age make a difference?

Support for inclusive language in the church is very clearly an age-related issue. While between two fifths and half of the women deacons in the oldest cohort in the study are supportive of the use of inclusive language in service books, bible translations and hymns, the support steadily increases through the younger cohorts. The following statistics illustrate the point.

Support for the use of inclusive language in service books rose from 54% among the women deacons aged sixty or over to 71% among the women deacons in their fifties, to 83% among the women deacons in their forties, and to 86% among the women deacons aged under forty. Support for the use of inclusive language in hymns rose from 46% among the women deacons aged sixty or over to 59% among the women deacons in their fifties, to 65% among the women deacons in their forties, and to 74% among the women deacons aged under forty. Support for the use of inclusive language in bible translations rose from 41% among the women deacons aged sixty or over to 60% among the women deacons in their fifties, to 67% among the women deacons in their forties, and to 67% among the women deacons aged under forty.

Support for the use of female imagery for God in both hymns and prayers is even more starkly related to age than support for inclusive language in church. Among the women deacons aged sixty or over just one in five (19%) was in favour of the use of female imagery for God in hymns and prayers. Among the women deacons in their forties the level of support had almost doubled to 35%. Among the women deacons aged under forty the level of support had almost trebled to 55%.

While support for inclusive language in church services has clearly grown with each successive cohort of women deacons, the perception that this is a controversial issue for local churches has remained fairly consistent. For example, 49% of the women deacons aged sixty or over considered that the use of inclusive language would be controversial in most congregations, and so did 52% of the women deacons aged under forty.

Does marital status make a difference?

Overall the married women deacons held a more positive attitude toward inclusive language in church than the single women deacons. This point is illustrated by the following statistics. While 56% of the single women deacons maintained that inclusive language should be used in bible translations, the proportion rose to 64% among the married women deacons. While 59% of the single women deacons maintained that inclusive language should be used in hymns, the proportion rose to 64% among the married women deacons. While 72% of the single women deacons maintained that inclusive language should be used in service books, the proportion rose to 78% among the married women deacons.

The married women deacons also held a more positive attitude toward female imagery for God than the single women deacons. While 27% of the single women deacons maintained that hymns and prayers should use female imagery for God, the proportion rose to 40% among the married women deacons.

The widowed women deacons held a less positive attitude toward inclusive language in church than the single women deacons. The widowed women deacons were less likely than the single women deacons to think that inclusive language should be used in bible translations (46% compared with 56%), hymns (46% compared with 59%) and service books (59% compared with 72%). The widowed women deacons held a similar attitude toward female imagery for God as held by the single women deacons. Thus, 27% of the single women deacons believed that hymns and prayers should use female imagery for God, and so did 29% of the widowed women deacons.

In some ways the divorced women deacons held a more radical view than the married women deacons on inclusive language in the church. While 64% of the married women deacons supported inclusive language in hymns, the proportion rose to 69% among the divorced women deacons. While 64% of the married women deacons supported inclusive language in bible translations the proportion rose to 72% among the divorced women deacons.

In other ways the divorced women deacons held similar attitudes to those held by the married women deacons. Support for inclusive language in service books was given by 78% of the married women deacons and by 79% of the divorced women deacons. Support for female imagery for God in hymns and prayers was given by 40% of the married women deacons and by 39% of the divorced women deacons.

Overall, similar proportions of single (45%), married (47%) and widowed (48%) women deacons felt that the use of inclusive language would be controversial in most congregations. The proportion of divorced women deacons taking this view, however, rose to 54%.

Does church tradition make a difference?

The data demonstrate two significant differences in views on inclusive language between the women deacons who identified with the Catholic wing of the Anglican church and the women deacons who identified with the Evangelical wing.

The first difference concerns the use of inclusive language in bible translations. The Evangelical women deacons were a little more inclined to adopt a conservative position on this issue. While 65% of the women deacons on the Catholic wing supported the use of inclusive language in bible translations, the proportion fell somewhat to 57% among the women deacons on the Evangelical wing. Although the Evangelical women deacons were more conservative regarding the use of inclusive langue in bible translations, they were as supportive as the Catholic women deacons regarding the use of inclusive language in hymns (61% and 63%) and in service books (76% and 77%).

The second difference concerns the appropriate use of female imagery for God. Once again, the Evangelical women deacons were more inclined to adopt a conservative position on the issue. While 41% of the women deacons on the Catholic wing supported the use of female imagery for God in hymns and prayers, the proportion fell to 29% among the women deacons on the Evangelical wing.

The women deacons who identified with the middle way of Anglicanism adopted a view on the use of female imagery for God midway between the Catholic women deacons and the Evangelical women deacons. Thus, 34% of the middle way women deacons supported the use of female imagery for God in both hymns and prayers, compared with 29% of the Evangelical women deacons and 41% of the Catholic women deacons.

On the other hand, the women deacons who identified with the middle way of Anglicanism adopted a less positive attitude toward inclusive language in service books than either the Catholic women deacons or the Evangelical women deacons. Thus, 71% of the middle way women deacons supported the use of inclusive language in service books, compared with 76% of the Evangelical women deacons and 77% of the Catholic women deacons.

Overall, similar proportions of Catholic (45%), middle way (48%) and Evangelical (47%) women deacons felt that the use of inclusive language would be controversial in most congregations.

Are non-stipendiaries different?

Stipendiary women deacons displayed a higher level of support for inclusive language in the church than was the case among non-stipendiary women deacons. This difference is clearly illustrated by the following statistics.

Four fifths (80%) of the stipendiary women deacons maintained that inclusive language should be used in service books, compared with 66% of the non-stipendiary women deacons. Two thirds (65%) of the stipendiary women deacons maintained that inclusive language should be used in bible translations, compared with 52% of the non-stipendiary women deacons. Two thirds (65%) of the stipendiary women deacons maintained that inclusive language should be used in hymns, compared with 51% of the non-stipendiary women deacons. Over a third (36%) of the stipendiary women deacons maintained that hymns and prayers should use female imagery for God, compared with 28% of the non-stipendiary women deacons.

Overall, similar proportions of the stipendiary women deacons (46%) and the non-stipendiary (47%) women deacons felt that the use of inclusive language would be controversial in most congregations.

Hearing the stories

The women deacons held a contrasting range of opinions on the issue of inclusive language. Listening to the views of these women deacons on inclusive language highlights four main areas.

First, there were those women deacons for whom inclusive language was not a live issue. This group of women deacons, however, was driven by two very different reasons. On the one hand, inclusive language was not a live issue because it was already used and accepted in their parish, as this woman deacon states.

> Fairly liberal place on the whole and we use inclusive language in the services with no complaints. *(stipendiary, assistant curate aged 43)*

On the other hand, inclusive language was not a live issue because they saw no point in its use, as is made clear by this woman deacon's view.

> I have always been part of mankind and all men. *(non-stipendiary, parish deacon aged 57)*

Second, for those women deacons who were looking to introduce or who were in the process of introducing inclusive language the problems resided in the best way of achieving this. For example, some felt that inclusive language should only be used in new hymns and prayers because congregations would otherwise have problems in coping.

> It would be disturbing to congregations to have too much altered in what is helpfully familiar. *(stipendiary, parish deacon aged 63)*

Third, a number of women made a clear distinction between the use of inclusive language in reference to God and its use in other areas. This view is summed up by the following woman deacon.

> I understand inclusive language as applying to humans not God *(retired, honorary parish deacon aged 70)*

Finally, for the majority of women deacons it was felt that inclusive language was important, but that it should be introduced gradually into parish life.

> Inclusive language should be introduced gradually and with explanation. *(stipendiary, assistant curate aged 42)*

19 Church's attitude to women

Introduction

Women ordained to the diaconate in the Church of England between 1987 and 1992 entered clerical ministry in a church which remained fundamentally unsure about the ordination of women to the priesthood. The issue regarding whether or not women would be ordained as priests within the Church of England was a major focus of attention, debate and controversy. What kind of messages were being communicated to the women deacons by this situation?

The aim of the present chapter is to assess the women deacons' interpretation of the church's attitude toward women. To what extent did they feel that the Church of England did not actively encourage women to ordained ministry? Or, having been ordained, did they feel that the Church of England discouraged women deacons from applying for jobs with a high profile? How many of them felt that the Church of England's attitude to women deacons challenged their vocation or made them question their own calling?

In another sense it is likely that the Church of England's uncertain attitude toward the ordination of women may have made difficulties for women deacons in some areas of their work. To what extent did the women deacons feel this to be the case, especially as this affected their work with men and with women differently?

Overview

The survey results show that a third (33%) of the women deacons considered that the Church of England did not actively encourage women to ordination. The proportion rose to more than half the women deacons (55%) who considered that the Church of England did not encourage women deacons to apply for high profile jobs. While two in five (43%) of the women deacons challenged the notion that the Church of England did not actively encourage women to ordination, fewer than one in five (18%) of the women deacons was willing to challenge the notion that the Church of England did not encourage women deacons to apply for jobs with a high profile. It is clear from these statistics that many women deacons were very conscious of the inferior status which they held in the church.

Table 19 Church's attitude to women

	Yes %	? %	No %
The Church of England:			
does not actively encourage women to ordained ministry	33	24	43
does not encourage women clergy to apply for jobs with a high profile	55	27	18
attitude to women clergy challenges my vocation	33	16	52
stance on the ordination of women makes me question my own calling	26	9	65
attitude to women clergy makes my work with women more difficult	9	12	79
attitude to women clergy makes my work with men more difficult	12	16	72

For one in every three (33%) of the women deacons the church's attitude to women clergy posed a challenge to her vocation. For one in every four (26%) of the women deacons the Church of England's stance on the ordination of women had made her go so far as to question her own calling. It is clear from these statistics that the confidence of many women deacons in themselves was being undermined by the church's attitude toward women.

A significant minority of the women deacons also felt that the church's attitude toward women deacons made aspects of their ministry more difficult, especially among men. Thus, 12% of the women deacons were clear that the church's attitude to women clergy made their work with men more difficult, while 9% of the women deacons were clear that the church's attitude to women clergy made their work with women more difficult. Looked at from another perspective, the proportion rose to 28% of the women deacons who suspected that the church's attitude may have had a negative impact on their work with men, and to 21% of the women deacons who suspected that the church's attitude may have had a negative impact on their work with women. It is clear from these statistics that the confidence of some women deacons in their ministry was being undermined by the church's attitude toward women.

Does age make a difference?

The extent to which the women deacons were made to question their own calling by the Church of England's stance on the ordination of women was directly related to the years of ministry they had stretching before them. While one in five (20%) of the women deacons aged sixty or over said that the Church of England's stance on the ordination of women made her question her own calling, the proportions gradually increased to 24% among the women deacons in their fifties, to 29% among the women deacons in their forties, and to 32% among the women deacons aged under forty.

In other areas the trend with age is less clear, although the contrast remains strongest between the youngest and the oldest cohorts. For example, while 27% of the women deacons aged sixty or over considered that the Church of England did not actively encourage women to ordained ministry, the proportion rose to 32% among the women deacons aged under forty. While half (48%) of the women deacons aged sixty or over considered that the Church of England did not encourage women clergy to apply for jobs with a high profile, the proportion rose to 59% among the women deacons aged under forty.

The youngest cohort of women deacons was also more inclined than the oldest cohort to feel that the church's attitude to women clergy made their job more difficult. For example, while 7% of the women deacons aged sixty or over considered that the church's attitude to women clergy made their work with women more difficult, the proportion rose to 15% among the women deacons aged under forty. Similarly, while 11% of the women deacons aged sixty or over considered that the church's attitude to women clergy made their work with men more difficult, the proportion rose to 15% among the women deacons aged under forty.

Does marital status make a difference?

Overall the married women deacons displayed somewhat greater discontent with the church's attitude toward women than was the case among the single women deacons. The married women deacons were more inclined than the single women deacons to take the view that the Church of England did not actively encourage women to ordained ministry (34% compared with 29%). The married women deacons were more inclined than the single women deacons to take the view that the Church of England did not encourage women clergy to apply for jobs with a high profile (57% compared with 53%).

Consistent with this trend, the married women deacons were somewhat more inclined than the single women deacons to feel their own calling undermined by the church. While 24% of the single women deacons felt that the Church of England's stance on the ordination of women made them question their own calling, the proportion rose to 28% among the married women deacons. While 28% of the single women deacons felt that the church's attitude to women clergy challenged their vocation, the proportion rose to 34% among the married women deacons.

On the other hand, married and single women deacons shared similar perceptions regarding the impact of the church's attitude on their own ministry. Thus, 9% of the single women deacons considered that the church's attitude to women clergy made their work with women more difficult, and so did 9% of the married women deacons. Similarly, 12% of the single women deacons considered that the church's attitude to women clergy made their work with men more difficult, and so did 11% of the married women deacons.

In many ways the profile of the widowed women deacons followed the profile of the single women deacons on this issue. For example, 29% of the single women deacons took the view that the Church of England did not actively encourage women to ordained ministry, and so did 27% of the widowed women deacons.

Overall, it is the divorced women deacons who displayed the highest level of dissatisfaction with the church's attitude to women. For example, 46% of the divorced women deacons agreed that the Church of England did not actively encourage women to ordained ministry, compared with 29% of the single women deacons and 34% of the married women deacons. Similarly, 61% of the divorced women deacons took the view that the Church of England did not encourage women clergy to apply for jobs with a high profile, compared with 53% of the single women deacons and 57% of the married women deacons.

The divorced women deacons were more inclined to feel that the church's attitude to women hampered their work. Thus, 18% of the divorced women deacons felt that the church's attitude to women made their work with women more difficult, compared with 9% of the single women deacons and 9% of the married women deacons. Similarly, 23% of the divorced women deacons felt that the church's attitude to women made their work with men more difficult, compared with 12% of the single women deacons and 11% of the married women deacons.

Consistent with this trend, the divorced women deacons were most likely to feel that the church's attitude to women challenged their vocation. While 28% of the single women deacons and 34% of the married women deacons said that the church's attitude to women clergy challenged their vocation, the proportion rose to 39% among the divorced women deacons.

Does church tradition make a difference?

The women deacons who identified with the Catholic wing of the church showed greater discontent with the church's attitude to women than the women deacons who identified with the Evangelical wing of the church. The Catholic women deacons were more inclined than the Evangelical women deacons to feel that the Church of England did not actively encourage women to ordained ministry (36% compared with 30%). The Catholic women deacons were also more inclined than the Evangelical women deacons to feel that the Church of England did not encourage women clergy to apply for jobs with a high profile (58% compared with 51%).

Consistent with this trend, the women deacons who identified with the Catholic wing of the church were more inclined than the women deacons who identified with the Evangelical wing of the church to feel their calling undermined by the church's attitude to women. Two out of every five (39%) of the Catholic women deacons reported that the church's attitude to women clergy challenged their vocation, compared with 27% of the Evangelical women deacons.

In many ways the women deacons who identified with the middle way of Anglicanism adopted a position on this issue between the Catholic women deacons and the Evangelical women deacons. Thus, 32% of the middle way women deacons felt their vocation to be challenged by the church's attitude to women clergy, compared with 27% of the Evangelical women deacons and 39% of the Catholic women deacons.

Church tradition did not make a significant impact on the proportion of women deacons who considered that the church's attitude to women clergy made their work with men or women more difficult.

Are non-stipendiaries different?

In some ways the non-stipendiary women deacons felt slightly more alienated than the stipendiary women deacons by the church's attitude to women. For example, the non-stipendiary women deacons were more likely than the stipendiary women deacons to feel that the Church of England did not actively encourage women to ordained ministry (34% compared with 30%). The non-stipendiary women deacons were more likely than the stipendiary women deacons to feel that the church's attitude to women clergy challenged their vocation (36% compared with 31%).

In other ways, however, there were no discernable differences between the non-stipendiary and stipendiary women deacons in this part of the survey.

Hearing the stories

Listening to the women deacons describe the church's attitude to them and to their ministry, it is clear that the church was not heard to speak with one voice. For some women deacons the church's attitude had been positive, for other women deacons the church's attitude had been negative, while for the majority it has been mixed. In their personal stories the women deacons highlighted four main areas where the church's attitude toward women had caused problems and difficulties.

First, their stories made it clear that some women deacons saw the church's policy as promoting discrimination against women in ministry. One woman deacon voiced this issue as follows.

> All the male colleagues with whom I was ordained are now incumbents whilst I am still in my first curacy. Such discrimination would certainly not be tolerated in secular employment. *(stipendiary, cathedral clergy aged 28)*

There were also stories of more subtle forms of discrimination. One woman deacon found herself in the following situation.

> My first appointment as a deacon was full-time, but paid as a part-time deacon. I have met other women deacons for whom this was the norm also. I don't think I've ever met a male cleric in this position. *(stipendiary, parish deacon aged 45)*

Second, their stories pointed to ways in which remuneration could be a problem for women deacons. One woman deacon gave the following account of her situation.

> As regards parish expenses, women are discriminated against, many male officials seeing our work as a hobby to keep us out of mischief. *(stipendiary, assistant curate aged 40)*

Third, their stories pointed to ways in which the church did not seem to be adequately prepared for dealing with issues that it faced in respect of women in ministry. Several women deacons suggested that clearly defined policies and parameters would help both men and women to work more effectively together. This point is summarised effectively as follows.

> The church needs policy in relation to women, e.g. diocesan equal opportunities policies (there is a lack of them), maternity policies and their effects on ministry. *(stipendiary, team minister aged 33)*

Fourth, their stories pointed to the specific problem in the church's attitude confronting some women deacons married to male priests. As this woman deacon pointed out, the church's attitude on this issue was causing difficulties for her own ministry and that of her husband.

> Because I am involved in full-time parish ministry my husband is experiencing difficulty in moving to a more challenging parish (i.e. it is perceived I could not fulfil clergy wife roles). *(stipendiary, assistant curate aged 33)*

20 Ordination debate

Introduction

At the time when the survey was underway, the implications of the debate regarding the ordination of women to the priesthood were being widely discussed both within the church and by the media. While some within the church were preparing carefully for the first services to ordain women to the priesthood, others were actively trying to challenge the decision of the General Synod or making plans to leave the Church of England. The whole controversy continued to be given a high profile by the religious and secular press. Public perception beyond the church in particular was being informed by the media. What impact was the media's attention having on the women deacons themselves?

This chapter sets out to assess the perceptions of the women deacons to two key aspects of the ordination debate. The first aspect concerns the impact of the media. To what extent did the women deacons feel that the media was treating the debate fairly, or did they feel that the media's attention was focused too heavily on the opponents to women priests? More generally, did the women deacons feel that the media attention was helpful to the public image of the church, or detrimental to it?

The second aspect concerns the attitude of the women deacons to the opponents to the ordination of women to the priesthood. How much did the women deacons try to understand the viewpoint of those who could not accept that women are called by God to the priesthood? How accepting were they of those who took this position? How difficult did they find it to cope with those who could not accept that women could be called to the priesthood by God?

Overview

The survey results show that four out of every five (78%) of the women deacons were convinced that the media's attention was too heavily focused on the opponents to women priests, while less than one in ten (8%) thought that this was an overstatement. There was, however, considerably less consensus among the women deacons regarding the general implications of the media attention for the church as a whole. While 29% of the women deacons considered that the media attention focused on the ordination of women as priests was detrimental to the church, another 46% clearly thought that this was not the case. What the statistics do make clear is that the women deacons did not feel the media to be on their side.

Table 20 Ordination debate

	Yes %	? %	No %
The media's attention is too heavily focused on the opponents to women priests	78	13	8
All the media attention to the Church of England ordaining women as priests is detrimental to the church	29	25	46
I try to be understanding of those who cannot accept that women are called by God to the ordained ministry as priests	92	6	2
I understand why some people cannot accept women in the ordained ministry as priests	75	13	12
I find it difficult to cope with those who cannot accept that women can be called to the priesthood by God	38	11	52

The survey results also show that the majority of women deacons took a generous attitude toward those who opposed the ordination of women to the priesthood. Three quarters (75%) of the women deacons said that they could understand why some people could not accept women as priests. The proportion rose to 92% of the women deacons who said that they tried to understand those who cannot accept that women are called by God to the ordained ministry of the priesthood. These statistics make it clear that the women deacons were very far from adopting a toughminded or militant stance against those who opposed their ordination to the priesthood.

In spite of adopting this generous attitude toward the opponents of the ordination of women to the priesthood, many women deacons needed to face the fact that such generosity was costly in personal terms. Two out of every five (38%) of the women deacons confessed that they found it difficult to cope with those who could not accept that women can be called to the priesthood by God.

Does age make a difference?

Close analysis of the responses of the four cohorts of women deacons (those under the age of forty, those in their forties, those in their fifties, and those aged sixty or over) to the ordination debate reveals two main trends.

The first trend concerns the way in which the women deacons viewed the media. The women deacons in their forties took a somewhat more negative view of the media treatment of the ordination debate than either their younger or their older colleagues. For example, 82% of the women deacons in their forties considered that the media's attention was too heavily focused on the opponents to women priests, compared with 77% of the women deacons under the age of forty, 79% of the women deacons in their fifties, and 72% of the women deacons aged sixty or over. Similarly, 35% of the women deacons in their forties considered that the media attention given to the controversy over the ordination of women as priests was detrimental to the church, compared with 22% of the women deacons under the age of forty, 28% of the women deacons in their fifties, and 30% of the women deacons aged sixty or over.

The second trend concerns the attitude of the women deacons toward the opponents to the ordination of women to the priesthood. The older women deacons found it somewhat easier than their younger colleagues to accept those who stood in the way of the path to priesthood. While 29% of the women deacons aged sixty or over found it difficult to cope with those who could not accept that women can be called to the priesthood by God, the proportions increased to 37% among the women deacons in their fifties, to 38% among the women deacons in their forties, and to 45% among the women deacons aged under forty. While four fifths (80%) of the women deacons aged sixty or over could understand why some people could not accept women in the ordained ministry as priests, the proportion fell to two thirds (67%) among the women deacons aged under forty. While 95% of the women deacons aged sixty or over tried to be understanding of those who could not accept that women are called by God to the ordained ministry as priests, the proportion fell to 88% among the women deacons aged under forty.

Does marital status make a difference?

The responses of the single women deacons differed from the responses of the married women deacons in three ways. The single women deacons were slightly less inclined than the married women deacons to consider that the media attention was too heavily focused on the opponents to women priests (76% compared with 80%). The single women deacons were much more likely than the married women deacons to consider that the media attention to the ordination of women as priests was detrimental to the church (36% compared with 26%). The single women deacons were slightly more inclined than the married women deacons to find it difficult to cope with those who could not accept that women can be called to the priesthood by God (41% compared with 37%).

The responses of the widowed women deacons differed from the responses of the married women deacons in two ways. The widowed women deacons were less inclined than the married women deacons to consider that the media attention was too heavily focused on the opponents to women priests (71% compared with 80%). The widowed women deacons were less inclined than the married women deacons to find it difficult to cope with those who could not accept that women can be called to the priesthood by God (31% compared with 37%).

The responses of the divorced women deacons differed from the responses of the married women deacons in two ways. The divorced women deacons were less inclined than the married women deacons to consider that the media attention to the ordination of women as priests was detrimental to the church (21% compared with 26%). The divorced women deacons were less inclined than the married women deacons to find it difficult to cope with those who could not accept that women can be called to the priesthood by God (33% compared with 37%).

Does church tradition make a difference?

The women deacons aligned with the Catholic wing of the church were more inclined than the women deacons aligned with the Evangelical wing of the church to complain that the media's attention was too heavily focused on the opponents to women priests (82% compared with 74%). On the other hand, the women deacons aligned with the Evangelical wing of the church were more inclined than the women deacons aligned with the Catholic wing of the church to complain that media attention given to the ordination of women as priests was detrimental to the church (32% compared with 28%).

The women deacons aligned with the middle way of Anglicanism took an attitude toward the media similar to the women deacons aligned with the Catholic wing. For example, 28% of the Catholic women deacons agreed that the media attention given to the ordination of women as priests was detrimental to the church, and so did 27% of the middle way women deacons. Four fifths (82%) of the Catholic women deacons agreed that the media's attention was too heavily focused on the opponents to women priests, and so did 79% of the middle way women deacons.

Overall, the Catholic women deacons, the Evangelical women deacons and the middle way women deacons displayed similar levels of tolerance toward the opponents to the ordination of women to the priesthood. For example, 90% of the Catholic women deacons tried to be understanding of those who could not accept that women are called by God to the ordained ministry as priests, and so did 93% of the Evangelical women deacons and 92% of the middle way women deacons. Taken from the opposite perspective, 36% of the Catholic women deacons found it difficult to cope with those who could not accept that women can be called to the priesthood by God, and so did 38% of the Evangelical women deacons and 39% of the middle way women deacons.

Are non-stipendiaries different?

Overall, the ordination debate seems to have impinged in very similar ways on the non-stipendiary women deacons and on the stipendiary women deacons. The present data show no significant differences between the two groups in response to this issue.

For example, 80% of the stipendiary women deacons maintained that the media's attention was too heavily focused on the opponents to women priests, and so did 80% of the non-stipendiary women deacons. Three in every ten stipendiary (31%) and non-stipendiary (29%) women deacons maintained that the media attention on the ordination of women was detrimental to the church. Between one third and two fifths of the stipendiary (38%) and non-stipendiary (36%) women deacons found it difficult to cope with those who could not accept that women can be called to the priesthood by God. Taken from the opposite perspective, 94% of the stipendiary and 93% of the non-stipendiary women deacons tended to be understanding of those who could not accept that women are called by God to the ordained ministry as priests.

Hearing the stories

Listening to the personal stories of the women deacons with regard to the ordination debate highlights four main areas.

First, many of the women deacons, although pleased that the Church of England had cleared the way for them to fulfil their vocation as priests, nonetheless expressed sadness at the division caused by the process. One woman deacon explained her position as follows.

> Sadness at divisions for those unable to accept women as priests. *(non-stipendiary, parish deacon aged 44)*

As a consequence of the division caused, some women deacons were holding back on seeking ordination to the priesthood. One woman deacon explained her position as follows.

> I shall not at present seek ordination to the priesthood because my vicar and a number of the congregation are not in favour of the ordination to the priesthood. I find their attitude to the present situation very hurtful. *(non-stipendiary, parish deacon aged 66)*

Second, there was also the recognition that as the reality of women priests grew clearer, new problems were arising even among those colleagues who support the ministry of women.

> I and female clergy are beginning to discover, as our ordination to the priesthood draws nearer, that male clergy who intellectually support women priests are beginning to show signs of anxiety about actually standing on equal ground with us. *(stipendiary, parish deacon aged 40)*

Third, many women deacons were growing very conscious of the expectations people would place on them as priests. The fear was that it would not be possible to live up to such high expectations, as this woman deacon states.

> If people think women priests are going to make a vast difference, they should not hold their breath. Don't put us on a pedestal. We're human beings with all our own frailties. *(stipendiary, assistant curate aged 50)*

Fourth, some of the women deacons argued that there was a need for a continuation of the debate in respect of diaconal ministry for those women and men who continued to feel called to the diaconal ministry rather than the priesthood.

> The attitude of the church marginalises and makes invisible the very real ministry deacons give to God. The fact that there will be no post for me in my diocese as a deacon once others have been priested shows this. *(stipendiary, hospital chaplain aged 35)*

Some women deacons wishing not to be priested felt that they were under pressure to be priested. This situation was even harder for those who did not agree with the ordination of women to the priesthood. One woman deacon viewed the issue in the following way.

> People find it hard to see how I can be pro-women's ministry but not supporting General Synod's decision regarding priesting. *(stipendiary, assistant curate aged 31)*

21 Legislation and ecumenism

Introduction

When the General Synod passed the *Priests (ordination of women) Measure* a number of new possibilities and a range of new problems confronted the Church of England. The aim of this chapter is to assess the attitudes of the women deacons to the new legislation. In particular three specific issues are examined.

The first issue concerns the personal response of the women deacons to the positive outcome of the debate in the General Synod. What did this outcome do for their own sense of ministry and vocation?

The second issue concerns the way in which the women deacons regarded the safeguards imposed by the measure to protect the position of those who remained unhappy with the Church of England ordaining women to the priesthood. These safeguards made financial provisions for those clergymen who no longer felt able to function as priests within the Church of England, after women had been ordained to the priesthood. These safeguards also instituted a system of alternative episcopal oversight for the clergy and congregations who remained within the Church of England but who refused to accept the ministry of women as priests. To what extent did the women deacons regard these safeguards as acceptable measures? Or to what extent did they perceive these safeguards as discriminating against women?

The third issue concerns the way in which the women deacons perceived the implications of the *Priests (ordination of women) measure* for the relationships between the Church of England and other churches. What implications did the women deacons see for the Church of England's relationships with other churches in Britain which already ordained women, with other churches in the Anglican communion, and with the Roman Catholic Church?

Overview

Table 21 Legislation and ecumenism

	Yes %	? %	No %
Since the Church of England has passed the *Priests (ordination of women) Measure* I feel my own vocation has been confirmed	80	13	7
The safeguards imposed by the Church of England with the *Priests (ordination of women) Measure* are unacceptable	42	35	24
The safeguards imposed by the Church of England with the *Priests (ordination of women) Measure* is discriminating against women	63	24	13
The *Priests (ordination of women) Measure* strengthens the Church of England's relationship with other churches in Britain which already ordain women	88	10	2
The *Priests (ordination of women) Measure* strengthens the Church of England's relationship with other churches in the Anglican communion	72	24	5
The *Priests (ordination of women) Measure* has had a detrimental effect on the Church of England's relationship with the Roman Catholic church	19	35	46
The *Priests (ordination of women) Measure* will have a long-term detrimental effect on the Church of England's relationship with the Roman Catholic church	6	24	71

The survey results show that the *Priests (ordination of women) Measure* was seen as an appropriate affirmation of their vocation by the majority of women deacons. Four out of every five (80%) of the women deacons felt that their vocation had been confirmed when the General Synod passed the measure.

For the majority of women deacons, the safeguards built into the measure to protect the consciences of those opposed to the ordination of women to the priesthood revealed an undervaluing of the ministry of women. Almost two thirds (63%) of the women deacons saw these safeguards as discriminating against women. Two fifths (42%) of the women deacons went so far as to say that the safeguards were unacceptable. Looked at from another perspective, only 24% of the women deacons were clear that the safeguards were actually acceptable.

The majority of the women deacons (88%) said that the *Priests (ordination of women) Measure* had strengthened the Church of England's relationship with other churches in Britain which already ordained women. Many of the women deacons (72%) also accepted that the measure was a positive move in strengthening the Church of England's relationship with other churches in the Anglican communion.

The major area of anxiety concerning the future of ecumenism focused on the implications of the measure for the relationship between the Church of England and the Roman Catholic Church. Only a small proportion of the women deacons, however, agreed with this view. While just 19% of the women deacons thought that the measure had a detrimental effect on the Church of England's relationship with the Roman Catholic Church, the proportion fell to 6% who considered that such a detrimental effect would be long lasting.

Does age make a difference?

The cohort of women deacons least impressed by the legislation was the younger women under the age of forty. These were the women who had the longest to serve as priests under the new legislation. The following two comparisons demonstrate this point. While 44% of the women deacons in their fifties and 43% of the women deacons in their forties felt that the safeguards built into the measure to protect the consciences of those opposed to the ordination of women to the priesthood were plainly unacceptable the proportion rose to 48% among the women deacons aged under forty. While 81% of the women deacons in their fifties and 83% of the women deacons in their forties felt that their own vocation had been confirmed by the General Synod passing the measure, the proportion fell to 72% among the women deacons aged under forty.

On the other hand, the cohort of women deacons least troubled by the legislation was the older women aged sixty or over. These were the women who had the shortest time to serve under the new legislation. The following statistics demonstrate this point. Between two fifths and one half of the women deacons under the age of forty (48%), in their forties (43%) and in their fifties (44%) found the safeguards for those opposed to the ordination of women to the priesthood unacceptable. The proportion fell, however, to 27% among the women deacons aged sixty or over. About two thirds of the women deacons under the age of forty (67%), in their forties (66%) and in their fifties (64%) argued that these safeguards discriminated against women. The proportion fell, however, to 52% among the women deacons aged sixty or over.

The oldest cohort of women deacons was also the most positive about the way in which the legislation promoted relationships with other churches. Thus, 92% of the women deacons aged sixty or over considered the legislation to strengthen the Church of England's relationship with other churches in Britain which already ordained women, compared with 86% of the women deacons under the age of forty. Similarly 77% of the women deacons aged sixty or over considered the legislation to strengthen the Church of England's relationship with other churches in the Anglican communion, compared with 69% of the women deacons under the age of forty.

At the same time, the oldest cohort of women deacons was also slightly more pessimistic about the implications of the legislation for the relationship with Rome. Thus, 23% of the women deacons aged sixty or over considered the legislation to have a detrimental effect on the Church of England's relationship with the Roman Catholic Church, compared with 19% of the women deacons aged forty and under.

Does marital status make a difference?

The attitudes of the married women deacons toward the legislation differ from the attitudes of the single women deacons in two ways. First, the married women deacons were more likely than the single women deacons to feel that the safeguards designed to protect those opposed to the ordination of women to the priesthood were discriminatory against women (67% compared with 59%). Second, the married women deacons were less likely than the single women deacons to feel that the legislation had a detrimental effect on the Church of England's relationship with the Roman Catholic church (17% compared with 23%).

In other respects the attitudes of the married women deacons and the single women deacons were very close. For example, 79% of the single women deacons felt that their own vocation had been confirmed by the passing of the measure, and so did 80% of the married women deacons.

Overall, the attitude of the widowed women deacons toward the legislation was more positive than the attitudes of either the married women deacons or the single women deacons. For example, 88% of the widowed women deacons felt that their own vocation had been confirmed by the measure being passed, compared with 80% of the married women deacons and 79% of the single women deacons. Similarly 95% of the widowed women deacons considered that the legislation strengthened the Church of England's relationship with other churches in Britain which already ordained women, compared with 88% of the married women deacons and 88% of the single women deacons. Looked at from the opposite perspective, while 67% of the married women deacons and 59% of the single women deacons considered the safeguards incorporated within the measure were discriminating against women, the proportion fell to 53% among the widowed women deacons.

In some ways the most angry reception for the legislation came from the divorced women deacons. While two in every five of the single (39%), married (42%) and widowed (42%) women deacons described the safeguards incorporated within the measure as unacceptable, the proportion rose to half (49%) of the divorced women deacons.

Does church tradition make a difference?

There are four important differences between the ways in which the Catholic women deacons and the Evangelical women deacons responded to the *Priests (ordination of women) Measure*.

The first difference concerns the likelihood of having had their own calling strengthened by the legislation. The women deacons on the Catholic wing of the church were more likely than the women deacons on the Evangelical wing of the church to have felt their own vocation confirmed by the measure being passed in the General Synod (80% compared with 74%).

The second difference concerns the level of sympathy shown toward the safeguards incorporated in the measure to protect the interests of those opposed to the ordination of women to the priesthood. The women deacons on the Catholic wing of the church were more likely than the women deacons on the Evangelical wing of the church to be critical of these measures. Thus a higher proportion of the Catholic women deacons described these measures as unacceptable (45% compared with 34%) and as discriminatory against women (67% compared with 55%).

The third difference concerns the assessment of the implications of the measure for relationships between the Church of England and the Roman Catholic Church. The women deacons on the Evangelical wing of the church were more likely than the women deacons on the Catholic wing of the church to judge the effects of the measure as detrimental in this respect (25% compared with 18%).

The fourth difference concerns the assessment of the implications of the measure for relationships between the Church of England and other churches. On the one hand, the women deacons on the Evangelical wing of the church were more inclined than the women deacons on the Catholic wing of the church to endorse the view that the legislation strengthened the Church of England's relationship with other churches in Britain which already ordain women (91% compared with 82%). On the other hand, the women deacons on the Catholic wing of the church were more inclined than the women deacons on the Evangelical wing of the church to endorse the view that the legislation strengthened the Church of England's relationship with other churches in the Anglican communion (75% compared with 66%).

The women deacons aligned with the middle way of Anglicanism were as negative toward the safeguards incorporated in the measure as the women deacons on the Catholic wing of the church. Thus 44% of the middle way and 45% of the Catholic women deacons regarded the safeguards as unacceptable, while 66% of the middle way and 67% of the Catholic women deacons regarded the safeguards as discriminating against women.

On the other hand, the women deacons aligned with the middle way of Anglicanism shared the higher optimism of the Evangelical women deacons regarding the positive effect of the legislation on the relationship between the Church of England and other churches in Britain which already ordain women. Thus, 91% of the Evangelical women deacons and 90% of the middle way women deacons considered this to be the case, compared with 82% of the Catholic women deacons. On the other hand, the women deacons aligned with the middle way of Anglicanism shared the higher option of the Catholic women deacons regarding the lack of damage done by the legislation to the relationship between the Church of England and the Roman Catholic church. Thus 18% of the Catholic and 17% of the middle way women deacons considered the measure to be detrimental in this effect, compared with 25% of the Evangelical women deacons.

Of the three church traditions the women deacons aligned with the middle way of Anglicanism were the most likely to feel their own vocation confirmed by the legislation (83%, compared with 80% of the Catholics and 74% of the Evangelicals).

Are non-stipendiaries different?

The non-stipendiary women deacons were less likely than the stipendiary women deacons to feel angry about the safeguards incorporated in the measure to protect those opposed to the ordination of women to the priesthood. While 66% of the stipendiary women deacons called these safeguards discriminatory against women, the proportion taking this line among the non-stipendiary women deacons fell to 56%. While 45% of the stipendiary women deacons called these safeguards unacceptable, the proportion taking this line among the non-stipendiary women deacons fell to 34%.

The non-stipendiary women deacons were also slightly less likely than the stipendiary women deacons to feel excited by the measure. While 83% of stipendiary women deacons felt their own vocation confirmed by the measure, the proportion fell to 79% among non-stipendiary women deacons.

The non-stipendiary women deacons and the stipendiary women deacons took similar views regarding the implications of the measure for the relationship between the Church of England and other churches.

Hearing the stories

Listening to the personal stories told by the women deacons it became clear that their views regarding the legislation were mixed. In particular, three main perspectives came through with reference to the *safeguards* the legislation put in place for those who in conscience could not accept women priests.

First, there were those women deacons who viewed the *safeguards* as a necessary part in the success of the legislation passing through the General Synod.

> Safeguarding legislation was necessary, if the vote was to be passed - a necessary evil. *(stipendiary, team minister aged 39)*

Second, other women deacons clearly saw the *safeguards* as unnecessary, as this woman deacon stated.

> The safeguards offered to male priests are unacceptable, if they have a vocation, safeguards are unnecessary. *(non-stipendiary, assistant curate aged 65)*

Third, yet other women deacons saw *safeguards* as an indication of the General Synod being unsure in the step they had taken in admitting women to the priesthood.

> The safeguards in the ordination of women measure - the form of the safeguards is a tacit admission that the church is not certain that it has made the right decision. *(stipendiary, parish deacon aged 44)*

On a different issue, the majority of the women deacons did not see the ordination of women to the priesthood as having a detrimental effect on the Church of England's relationship with other churches at the grass roots level where things really mattered. This woman deacon's response is typical of that expressed in relation to the Roman Catholic Church.

> The hierarchy of the Roman Catholic Church differs from the Roman Catholic laity from whom I have had support. *(stipendiary, parish deacon aged 59)*

22 Bishops and beyond

Introduction

Passing the *Priests (ordination of women) Measure* may have been an important milestone in the recognition of the ministry of women within the Church of England by drawing to a close the long diaconate, but this is by no means the end of the journey. The final section of the survey was designed, therefore, to assess how the women deacons perceived the way ahead. In particular two issues were explored.

The first issue concerned the appointment of women clergy to senior positions in the church. Having at long last been accepted for ordination to the priesthood, how keen were the women deacons to see women clergy appointed to senior positions in the church? Then, how much do they envisage that the appointment of women clergy to senior positions in the church will be a cause of further controversy?

The second issue concerned the consecration of women as bishops within the Church of England. How willing were the women deacons to support the idea of women being appointed as bishops? Do they think that the appointment of women as bishops would be of benefit to the church? But, then, do they really think that women are likely to be consecrated as bishops in the Church of England within the near future?

Overview

The survey results show that the vast majority of the women deacons (90%) believed that women should now be appointed to senior positions in the church. Only two women deacons in every hundred (2%) actively dissented from this view. At the same time, between two and three times as many women deacons anticipated that such appointments would prove controversial as imagined that such appointments would take place smoothly. Thus, 55% of the women deacons agreed that the appointment of women to senior positions in the church would cause further controversy, compared with 22% who did not agree that this would be the case.

Table 22 Bishops and beyond

	Yes %	? %	No %
More women should be appointed to senior positions in the church	90	8	2
The appointment of women to senior positions in the church will cause further controversy	55	23	22
I have no objection to women being appointed bishops	91	7	2
The appointment of women as bishops would be of benefit to the church	80	18	2
I feel women will be consecrated as bishops in the Church of England within the next decade	45	38	17

The vast majority of the women deacons were also clearly in favour of women being appointed as bishops. Only 2% of the women deacons had objections to women being appointed as bishops, compared with 91% who had no objection at all. Indeed, four out of every five (80%) of the women deacons were convinced that appointing women as bishops would be of benefit to the church. In the aftermath of the General Synod passing the *Priests (ordination of women) Measure*, a good number of women deacons were optimistic that women would be consecrated as bishops in the Church of England within the next decade. As many as 45% thought this to be likely, compared with 17% who ruled it out as an impossibility.

Does age make a difference?

Views on the future development of the ministry of women within the Church of England were quite clearly age-related, with the sharpest contrast emerging between the youngest cohort (the women deacons aged under forty) and the oldest cohort (the women deacons aged sixty or over). The younger cohort is both more committed to the development of the ministry of women and less convinced that the church really wants the development. This same point is illustrated in relationship both to the appointment of women clergy to senior posts in the church and to the consecration of women as bishops.

The women deacons aged under forty were more inclined than their older colleagues to argue that more women clergy should be appointed to senior positions in the church (93%, compared with 90% of the women deacons in their forties, 90% of the women deacons in their fifties, and 87% of the women deacons aged sixty or over). The women deacons aged under forty were also more inclined than their older colleagues to feel that the appointment of women to senior positions in the church would cause further controversy (65%, compared with 57% of the women deacons in their forties, 54% of the women deacons in their fifties, and 42% of the women deacons aged sixty or over).

The women deacons aged under forty were more inclined than their older colleagues to argue that the appointment of women as bishops would be of benefit to the church (87%, compared with 81% of the women deacons in their forties, 79% of the women deacons in their fifties, and 70% of the women deacons aged sixty or over). At the same time, the women deacons aged under forty were less optimistic than their older colleagues that women would be made bishops in the near future. Thus, 37% of the women deacons aged under forty felt that women would be consecrated as bishops in the Church of England within the next decade, compared with 44% of the women deacons in their forties, 48% of the women deacons in their fifties, and 53% of the women deacons aged sixty or over.

Does marital status make a difference?

The married women deacons were generally more positive than the single women deacons in their view of the future for the ministry of women in the church. This is seen most clearly in their attitude toward the appointment of women bishops.

To begin with, the married women deacons were more likely than the single women deacons to say that they had no objections to women being appointed as bishops (93% compared with 86%). The married women deacons were more likely than the single women deacons to argue that the appointment of women as bishops would be of benefit to the church (83% compared with 74%). Finally, the married women deacons were more likely than the single women deacons to feel that women would be consecrated as bishops within the Church of England within the next decade (49% compared with 37%).

Similar proportions of married (91%) and single (89%) women deacons argued that women should be appointed to senior positions in the church. Married women deacons were, however, a little more likely than single women deacons to feel that such appointments would cause further controversy (57% compared with 53%).

Compared with the married women deacons, the widowed women deacons were personally less enthusiastic about the appointment of women as bishops but more convinced that this would actually happen. Thus, 88% of the widowed women deacons said that they had no objections to women being appointed as bishops, compared with 93% of the married women deacons. At the same time, 54% of the widowed women deacons felt that women would be consecrated as bishops in the Church of England within the next decade, compared with 49% of the married women deacons.

Of all the four groups, it is the divorced women deacons who showed the highest level of support for the consecration of women as bishops. Thus, 98% of the divorced women deacons said that they had no objections to women being appointed as bishops, compared with 93% of the married women deacons, 88% of the widowed women deacons, and 86% of the single women deacons. Similarly, 87% of the divorced women deacons argued that the appointment of women as bishops would be of benefit to the church, compared with 83% of the married women deacons, 80% of the widowed women deacons, and 74% of the single women deacons. At the same time, the divorced women deacons shared with the widowed women deacons a higher level of expectation that women would be consecrated as bishops in the Church of England within the next decade. This view was taken by 53% of the divorced and 54% of the widowed women deacons, compared with 49% of the married women deacons and 37% of the single women deacons.

Does church tradition make a difference?

The women deacons on the Catholic wing of the church held a more positive attitude toward the appointment of women as bishops than the women deacons on the Evangelical wing of the church. This difference is illustrated by the following statistics.

While 86% of the Evangelical women deacons said that they had no objection to women being appointed as bishops, the proportion rose to 94% among the Catholic women deacons. While 76% of the Evangelical women deacons felt that the appointment of women as bishops would be of benefit to the church, the proportion rose to 81% of the Catholic women deacons. While 40% of the Evangelical women deacons expected that women would be consecrated as bishops in the Church of England within the next decade, the proportion rose to 49% among the Catholic women deacons.

On the other hand, the Catholic women deacons and the Evangelical women deacons held very similar views on the appointment of women clergy to senior positions. For example, 90% of the Catholic women deacons argued that more women should be appointed to senior positions in the church, and so did 90% of the Evangelical women deacons. Similarly, 57% of the Catholic women deacons felt that the appointment of women to senior positions in the church would cause further controversy, and so did 57% of the Evangelical women deacons.

The women deacons who identified with the middle way of Anglicanism displayed a profile very close to that of the Catholic women deacons. For example, 94% of the middle way women deacons and 94% of the Catholic women deacons had no objection to women being appointed as bishops, while 48% of the middle way women deacons and 49% of the Catholic women deacons expected the Church of England to consecrate the first women bishops within the next decade.

Are non-stipendiaries different?

The stipendiary women deacons were more inclined than the non-stipendiary women deacons to argue in favour of the appointment of women as bishops, but less inclined to be optimistic about this happening soon. On the one hand, while 76% of the non-stipendiary women deacons argued that the appointment of women as bishops would be of benefit to the church, the proportion rose to 81% among the stipendiary women deacons. On the other hand, while 50% of the non-stipendiary women deacons felt that women would be consecrated as bishops in the Church of England within the next decade, the proportion fell to 42% among the stipendiary women deacons.

The stipendiary women deacons were slightly more inclined than the non-stipendiary women deacons to argue that more women should be appointed to senior positions in the church (91% compared with 87%). The two groups did not differ, however, over the amount of controversy this would cause. Thus, 55% of the stipendiary women deacons and 55% of the non-stipendiary women deacons felt that the appointment of more women to senior positions in the church would cause further controversy.

Hearing the stories

Listening to the voices of the women deacons on the issue of women bishops, it is clear that for the majority of women deacons the real question was not *whether* there would be women bishops but *when* there would be women bishops. Many women deacons felt that the real battle was to pass the *Priests (ordination of women) Measure* and, now that had been passed, women bishops would be the next logical step. The following women deacon spoke for many.

> I think there is an inevitability about the appointment of women as bishops, a natural progression deacon, priest, bishop. *(non-stipendiary, parish deacon aged 58)*

Some women deacons voiced the expectation that a woman bishop would change the perception of the role of bishop, and reconceptualise this role from a feminine perspective. One woman deacon summed up the view as follows.

> I hope that when we have women bishops they will change it, be bishops in their own right. *(stipendiary, assistant curate aged 42)*

Other women deacons, however, recognised that the possibility of such changes might give rise to all sorts of fears. One woman deacon said that her:

> incumbent is terrified that our next bishop will be Penny Jamieson. Absurd. *(non-stipendiary, parish deacon aged 59)*

A number of the women deacons expressed a wish not to enter the hierarchical structure of the church, but rather to change it from within.

> Both women and men need to work together to change the structure of power within the church. *(stipendiary, parish deacon aged 39)*

Other women deacons saw the appointment of women clergy to senior positions in the church clearly as a way of changing the church.

> I think it is important for women to offer themselves for senior positions in the church, only then can they change the church.
> *(non-stipendiary, assistant curate aged 61)*

Overall, there seemed to be little sense of urgency expresssed by the women deacons that legislation for women bishops should be pushed through quickly. However, it was clear from their stories that the women deacons needed to feel represented throughout the church structure with appropriate opportunities for responsibility and chances to apply for more senior posts.

Conclusion

The Long Diaconate set out to listen to the women who had been ordained deacon between 1987 and 1992, during those years when the Church of England remained uncertain whether it wished to ordain women to the priesthood. These are the women who lived through that uncertainty. The majority of them were ordained to the priesthood in 1994.

Their story is now being told five years later when the memory of those years is already beginning to fade, but before it has been totally forgotten. The first ordinations of women to the priesthood in 1994 seemed to some to have brought the journey to a close. Now five years later it is possible to stand back and to assess just how much progress has been made in accepting the ministry of women in the Church of England.

Our study was set up in 1993 to provide a benchmark against which changes brought about by the ordination of women to the priesthood could be assessed. We would like to repeat the study in 2004 to mark the tenth anniversary of these first ordinations. Then the findings from the two studies could be compared and a proper assessment could be made of the changes which have, or have not, taken place.

It is impossible to provide a succinct summary of the mass of data displayed and discussed in the body of this book. Nonetheless, it is both possible and desirable to point out some of the salient features from each of the twenty two key sections and to ask whether five years on these features still ring true.

The study began by examining the women deacons' *call to ministry*. The key statistic here is that nearly half of them (46%) reported that their gender had made it more difficult for them to seek ordination. Moreover, these were the women who had persisted with their vocation and survived the journey as far as the diaconate. Is this same story being repeated at the end of the 1990s and into the next millennium?

The study moved from the call to ministry to an examination of the *selection process*. The key statistic here is that nearly a quarter of the women deacons (23%) were unable to affirm that the selection process had been a positive experience for them. Once again, however, these were the women who had been recommended for training. According to the official statistics the proportion of candidates not recommended for training varied between 31% in 1978 to 48% in 1992, and those not recommended for training often feel less positive about the selection process. Is this same story being reported at the end of the 1990s and into the next millennium?

From the selection process the study moved to the *first appointment*. Many of the women deacons coming into their first appointment came as mature candidates for ministry with previous experience in another professional field. In that first appointment many felt undervalued, deskilled and under stretched. A third of the women deacons (32%) made the point that their first appointment did not make sufficient use of their talents. Is the same story being reported at the end of the 1990s and into the next millennium?

Crucial to making the most of the first appointment is the personal and professional relationship between the curate and the *training incumbent*. During the long diaconate all training incumbents were probably male priests, the majority of whom had been given no special training on adjusting their practice from working with male curates to working with female curates. Now gradually the situation is changing as more women priests move into senior posts of responsibility, but it is likely that the majority of women deacons may still be placed with male training incumbents. Two key statistics leap out from this section. One in five women deacons (20%) reported that her training incumbent felt uncomfortable working with a female colleague. One in five women deacons (20%) reported that her training incumbent's wife felt threatened by her. Is this same story being reported at the end of the 1990s and into the next millennium?

From their first appointment the study moved to their *last appointment as deacon*. Unlike their male colleagues who were priested and could then move more easily into situations of sole cure, throughout their long diaconate the women deacons could only move on from their initial training curacy into another curacy or to a post as parish deacon or team rector. In these situations they remained responsible to an incumbent. Now the ordination of women to the priesthood opens other possibilities to women priests. If, however, there is truth in the view that women clergy prefer forms of collaborative ministry it may still be the case that clergywomen are likely to continue seeking appointments in team ministries or as part of a clergy team. The key statistic from this section of the research is that well under half the women deacons (44%) considered that in their last appointment as deacon they had been given an equal share of the responsibility. Many felt that they were not fully involved in making decisions and that their talents remained under used. Is this same story being repeated at the end of the 1990s and into the next millennium?

Just as the personal and professional relationship between curate and training incumbent is crucial during the first appointment, so during their last appointment as deacon much hinged on the relationship with their *last incumbent as deacon*. The key problem at this stage in ministry was that a considerable cohort of women deacons, becoming well established in ministry and confident in their role, began to pose a threat to the authority and security of their male incumbents. Thus, one in five of the women deacons (22%) reported that her last incumbent as deacon felt threatened by her. Is this same story being repeated at the end of the 1990s and into the next millennium?

While the women deacons could properly hope that the parish in which they had been placed or where they chose to work was fully open to the ministry of women, they could not necessarily expect the same openness from *clerical colleagues* in the deanery chapter. One of the major hurts experienced by the women deacons concerned the feeling of rejection by their male colleagues. Now that women have been ordained to the priesthood the divisions within clergy chapters may be even more acutely felt and expressed. The key statistic from this section is that only a little over half the women deacons (56%) reported that they felt part of the professional life of other clergy in their area. Is this same story being repeated at the end of the 1990s and into the next millennium?

From the wider issue of clerical colleagues, the study moved closer to home to the women deacons' perceptions of their own *parishioners* and congregation. Here the picture is one of acceptance and welcome for those pioneers in women's ministry from the churches which accepted a woman deacon into the clergy staff. Two key statistics demand attention from this section. First, only one in twenty of the women deacons (5%) reported that her congregation was unhappy when she took up her present appointment because she was female. Second, over two thirds of the women deacons (69%) reported that their congregation have become more favourable to women in ministry since they took up their appointment. It is this kind of positive encouragement which could compensate for many set backs and hurts. Now, however, there is a larger number of women in ministry, the initial impact has been made, and in some places the determination of those opposed to the ordination of women has been strengthened. Can women clergy expect similar affirmation from congregations at the end of the 1990s and into the next millennium?

The balance between the professional commitments of ministry and the personal commitments to family life is increasingly recognised as a crucial issue for married male clergy. It was no less an issue for the married women deacons. There are two key statistics which stand out from this part of the survey. Just over half of the married women deacons (52%) reported that often they do not have enough time for their family. One in ten of the married women deacons (9%) reported that her partner was very resentful of the amount of time she spends on the job. Both of these statistics send out warnings about the stability of clergy marriages in face of pressures which can be generated by commitment to the job. Is this same story being repeated at the end of the 1990s and into the next millennium?

The demands and pressures of clerical life also place certain constraints on friendship patterns. On the one hand, clergy may be encouraged to keep their real and closest *friends* outside the parish. On the other hand, a busy parish life may find insufficient time to maintain and support friendships at a distance. In essence the debate is concerning the desirability of keeping private life and ministerial life separate. The key statistic in this section is that only two in every five of the women deacons (42%) reported that they were able to keep their private life and ministerial duties separate. Such a close identification between the personal and the professional may store up difficulties in the long term. Is this same story being repeated at the end of the 1990s and into the next millennium?

Some commentators have argued that women clergy, possibly more than male clergy, may prefer a *collaborative ministry* style. Evidence from the present survey adds support to this view, with three quarters of the women deacons (72%) reporting that they took other people's views fully into consideration in shaping their ministry. The danger with a collaborative ministry style is that some may perceive collaboration as a sign of weakness and try to exert pressure over clergy who operate in that way. The key statistic in this section is that one in ten of the women deacons (9%) reported that other people tried too hard to influence her ministry. Some may find such pressure overwhelming. There is a clear role for continuing ministerial education to equip clergy to deal with such pressures. Is this same story being repeated at the end of the 1990s and into the next millennium?

The next section on *stress in ministry* focused very clearly the signs of pressure emerging in the lives of women clergy. The key statistics in this section are that three out of every four women deacons reported that often they did not have enough time for themselves (72%) and that often they did not have enough time for their hobbies and interests (75%). Three out of every four women deacons also reported that they often imposed unrealistic expectations on themselves (74%). Unrealistic self expectations, coupled with overwork and lack of time for personal recreation, could easily lead to emotional exhaustion, physical tiredness, frustration and dissatisfaction. Such signs of warning need to be taken seriously. Once again there is a clear role for continuing ministerial education to help clergy to recognise stress and to develop techniques of stress management. Is this same story of clergy stress going to be repeated at the end of the 1990s and into the next millennium?

From a consideration of stress the survey turned to a consideration of *satisfaction in ministry*. The high levels of stress in ministry by no means imply low levels of satisfaction. This section of the survey confirms that the vast majority of the women deacons were going about their work with purpose and deriving considerable satisfaction from their ministry. Two key statistics demonstrate this point. Six out of every seven women deacons (86%) reported that they felt that they were accomplishing things in their ministry. Three out of every four women deacons (77%) reported that they felt that they were growing spiritually in their ministry. While these positive statistics, in some senses, offset the more negative statistics concerning stress, it may be a mistake to interpret them as a source for complacency. If figures of church attendance continue to decline into the next millennium, a serious threat may be posed to the sustainability of some of those signs of growth which lead to feelings of personal accomplishment. Is the same story of clergy satisfaction going to be repeated at the end of the 1990s, and into the next millennium?

The next four sections of the survey explored the perceptions of the women deacons regarding the comparative skills which women clergy and male clergy bring to ministry. In turn these sections explored the *public role*, the *pastoral role*, the *social role*, and the *liturgical role*. Some theoretical perspectives have argued not only that women bring different skills to ministry from those skills brought by men, but also that women are better than men in certain ministry areas. The four sections on the public, pastoral, social and liturgical roles in ministry offer three insights into this theoretical perspective.

The first insight is that, overall, only a relatively small proportion of the women deacons argued that women generally were better at ministry functions than men. For example, an average 12% of the women deacons considered that women clergy were better than male clergy at the public roles of ministry listed in the survey. On average 13% of the women deacons considered that women clergy were better than male clergy at the liturgical roles of ministry listed in the survey.

The second insight is that the women deacons differentiated quite clearly between those roles regarding which there was greater consensus regarding the particular contribution of women to ministry and other areas in which women clergy were not likely to be considered to be better than men. The roles in which the women deacons considered women clergy to be better than male clergy tended to conform to established stereotypes regarding the differences between men and women. The following key statistics demonstrate this point. Within the public role of ministry 27% of the women deacons considered women clergy to be better visitors than male clergy, while only 5% considered women clergy to be better preachers than male clergy. Such stereotyping of women's ministry may prove unhelpful for promoting full complementarity between the ministry of women and men. Will such stereotyping persist through the 1990s and into the next millennium?

The third insight is that the responses of the women deacons to this part of the survey differed considerably among the different age cohorts. The tendency to maintain gender stereotypes was much less among the younger women deacons than among the older women deacons. The following statistics demonstrate this point. Within the public role of ministry, the proportion of women deacons who maintained that women clergy were better visitors than male clergy dropped from 45%

among those aged sixty and over to 15% among those aged under forty. Within the pastoral role of ministry, the proportion of women deacons who maintained that women clergy were better than male clergy at bereavement counselling dropped from 46% among those aged sixty and over to 21% among those aged under forty. Within the social role of ministry, the proportion of women deacons who maintained that women clergy were better than male clergy at work with preschool children dropped from 46% among those aged sixty or over to 18% among those aged under forty. Within the liturgical role of ministry, the proportion of women deacons who maintained that women clergy were better than male clergy at conducting funerals dropped from 36% among those aged sixty and over to 18% among those aged under forty. These figures make it clear that in some senses at least the next generation of women clergy may have very different views on ministry from earlier generations of women clergy. Is the church likely to adjust its attitude to and expectation of women in ministry sufficiently to accommodate these changes through the 1990s and into the next millennium?

The Church of England has been comparatively slow to grasp the nettle of *inclusive language*. The impression is that this remains a divisive issue within congregations. The responses of the women deacons made two points clear on this issue. First, the women deacons themselves are basically committed to inclusive language. Three out of four of all the women deacons (75%) maintained that inclusive language should be used in service books, and the proportion rose to 86% among the women deacons aged under forty. Second, the women deacons were aware that inclusive language is a controversial issue. Half the women deacons (47%) recognised that the use of inclusive language will be controversial in most congregations. Will this battle over inclusive language persist through the 1990s and into the next millennium?

From inclusive language the survey moved to the broader issue of the *church's attitude to women*. Throughout the long diaconate the Church of England had sent out negative, or at best uncertain, signals over its attitude toward women in ministry. Two key statistics stand out concerning the responses of the women deacons to this situation. One in three of the women deacons (33%) reported that, in her view, the Church of England did not actively encourage women to ordained ministry. Having then ordained women to ministry, over half of the women deacons (55%) considered that the Church of England did not encourage women clergy to apply for jobs with a high profile. In one sense, the ordination of women to the priesthood may have overturned this negative perception. In another sense, however, continuing opposition to women priests within parts of the Church of England may only have served to reinforce this negative perception. Will women clergy perceive the Church of England to have developed a more positive attitude toward women through the 1990s and into the next millennium?

When the survey was conducted, the debate on the implications of the ordination of women to the priesthood was still being waged. Potentially this was a time of considerable trauma and hurt for women in ministry, as they witnessed their vocation to priesthood rejected by some and as they witnessed some of their male colleagues and bishops prepared to leave the Church of England over this divisive issue. The key statistic from this section of the survey emphasises the patience with which the majority of women clergy participated in the debate. Thus, 92% of the women deacons reported that they tried to be understanding of those who could not accept that women are called by God to the ordained ministry as priests. The need for patience clearly remains, as some clergy, some parishes and a new episcopal structure continue to brace themselves to stand against the priestly ministry of women. Will women clergy, however, continue to remain so patient and accepting through the 1990s and into the next millennium?

The *legislation* surrounding the ordination of women to the priesthood proved controversial for a number of reasons, and not least because of the safeguards imposed to protect the conscience of those opposed to the ordination of women to the priesthood. The responses to the survey showed that nearly two thirds of the women deacons (63%) felt that this aspect of the legislation was actually discriminating against women, while 42% went so far as to maintain that these provisions were unacceptable. Nonetheless, it is this legislation which has provided the context in which women currently exercise their ministry of priesthood within the Church of England. As the Church of England enters the next millennium will this attitude of hurt among women clergy continue to persist?

The final section of the survey, *Bishops and beyond*, focused on the vision of the women deacons for the future. Having at long last had their vocation to priesthood recognised and vindicated by the Church of England, these women deacons were in buoyant mood and saw no reason why ordination to the priesthood should mark the end of the journey. The statistics show that nine out of ten of the women deacons (90%) believed that from now on more women should be appointed to senior positions in the church. Nine out of ten of the women deacons (91%) had no objection to women being appointed bishops. Nearly half of the women deacons (45%) felt that women would be consecrated as bishops in the Church of England before 2004. Can such aspirations continue to hold up through the 1990s and into the next millennium?

The foregoing careful analysis of the attitudes and views of women deacons within the Church of England immediately prior to the ordination of women to the priesthood focuses and clarifies a clear range of questions regarding the way in which the ministry of women is shaping during the 1990s and into the next millennium. The data from the present study can also provide the essential benchmark against which change can be assessed. This is one of the unique contributions which studies in empirical theology can make to understanding ministry and to the developing life of the church.

Endnotes

1. According to *Church Statistics*, 1989, a total of 103 women were ordained deacon in 1987.
2. For discussions of the diaconate in the Church of England following the admission of women to the order of deacon in 1987, see the ACCM report *Deacons Now: the report of a Church of England working party concerned with women in ordained ministry*, London, ACCM, 1990. See also C. Hall (ed.), *The Deacon's Ministry*, Leominster, Gracewing, 1991. It is interesting to note that once the *Priests (ordination of women) measure* was passed discussions in respect of permanent diaconate largely ceased on an official church level.
3. See, for example, *Deacons in the Ministry of the Church*, a report to the House of Bishops of the General Synod of the Church of England (GS802), London, Church House Publishing, 1988. This report became known as *The Portsmouth Report*. The Portsmouth Scheme aimed to restore the permanent diaconate within that one diocese with limited long term success.
4. The first ordinations of women as priests took place at Bristol Cathedral on March 12 1994. A total of 32 women were ordained on that day.
5. See, for example, *Church Statistics: some facts and figures about the Church of England: 1989*, London, Central Board of Finance of the Church of England, 1989.
6. S.W. Cardwell, Why women fail/succeed in ministry: psychological factors, *Pastoral Psychology*, 30, pp 153-162, 1982.
7. R.A. Hunt, S.W. Cardwell and J.E. Dittes, *Theological School Inventory Manual and Guide to Interpreting the TSI*, Dallas, Texas, Ministry Studies Board, 1976.
8. *MMPT Interpretation Manual for Counsellors and Clinicians* (2nd edition), Maunce, Indiana, Accelerated Development Inc, 1979.
9. H.G. Gough and A.B. Heilbrun Jr, *Adjective Check List Manual*, Palo Alto, California, Consulting Psychologists Press, 1965.
10. E.T. Sullivan, W.W. Clark and E.W. Tiegs, *Examiners Manual California Short-Form Test of Mental Maturity*, Monterey, California, McGraw-Hill Inc, 1963.
11. J.W. Carroll, B. Hargrove and A.T. Lummis, *Women of the Cloth: a new opportunity for the churches*, New York, Harper and Row, 1983.
12. M. Coger, *Women in Parish Ministry Stress and Support*, New York, The Alban Institute, 1985.
13. D.C. Carpenter, The professionalization of the ministry of women, *Journal of Religious Thought*, 43, pp 59-75, 1987.
14. M. Long Ice, *Clergywomen and their World Views: calling for a new age*, London, Praeger, 1987.
15. P.D. Nesbitt, Dual ordination tracks: differential benefits and costs for men and women clergy, *Sociology of Religion*, 54, pp 13-30, 1993.
16. *Presbyterian Clergywomen Survey: final report*, produced by Presbyterian Church Research Services, Louisville, Kentucky, USA, 1993.

17 Y. Amir, Contact hypothesis in ethnic relations, *Psychological Bulletin*, 71, pp 319-342, 1969.
18 E.C. Lehman Jr has produced a number of studies in relation to this issue in the USA, see for example Patterns of lay resistance to women in ministry, *Sociological Analysis*, 41, pp 317-338, 1981 or Research on lay church members attitudes toward women clergy: an assessment, *Review of Religious Research*, 28, 319-329, 1987. J.W. Carroll, B. Hargrove and A.T. Lummis, *Women of the Cloth: a new opportunity for the churches*, New York, Harper and Row, 1983.
19 E.C. Lehman Jr, Organisational resistance to women in ministry, *Sociological Analysis*, 42, pp 101-118, 1981.
20 M.H. Royle, Women pastors, what happens after placement? *Review of Religious Research*, 24, pp 116-126, 1982.
21 W.E. Bock, The female clergy: a case of professional marginality, in A. Theodore (ed.), *Professional Women*, pp 599-611, Cambridge, Massachusetts, Schenkman Publishing Company Inc., 1971. See also Bock's article in *American Journal of Sociology*, 27, pp 531-539, 1967, of the same name.
22 H.N. Malony, Men and women in the clergy: stresses, strains and resources, *Pastoral Psychology*, 36, pp 164-168, 1988.
23 E.C. Lehman Jr, *Gender and Work: the case of the clergy*, New York, State University of New York Press, 1993.
24 K. Flagg, Psychological androgyny and self-esteem in clergywomen, *Journal of Psychology and Theology*, 12, pp 222-229, 1984.
25 R. Helmreich, J. Stapp and C. Ervin, The Texas Social Behaviour Inventory (TSBI): an objective measure of self-esteem or social competence, *Journal Supplement Abstract Service: Catalogue of Selected Documents in Psychology*, 79, Ms No. 681, 1974.
26 S.L. Bem, *Bem Sex Role Inventory: professional manual*, Palo Alto, California, Consulting Psychologists Press, 1981.
27 B.N. Ekhardt and W. M. Goldsmith, Personality factors of men and women pastoral candidates Part I: motivational profiles, *Journal of Psychology and Theology*, 12, pp 109-118, 1984.
28 D.N. Jackson, *Personality Research Form*, Goshen, New York, 1974.
29 Advisory Council for the Church's Ministry, *Deacons Now: the report of a Church of England working party concerned with women in ordained ministry*, London, ACCM, 1990.
30 S. Penfold, *Women in Ministry*, Crowborough, Highland Books, 1991.
31 C. Treasure, *Walking on Glass: women deacons speak out*, London, SPCK, 1991.
32 See for example W.C. Roof, The local cosmopolitan orientation and traditional religious commitment, *Sociological Analysis*, 33, pp 1-15, 1972; Religious orthodoxy and minority prejudice: causal relationship or reflecting localistic world view? *American Journal of Sociology*, 80, pp 643-664, 1974; Traditional religion in contemporary society: a theory of local cosmopolitan plausibility, *American Sociological Review*, 41, pp 195-205, 1976.

33 E.C. Lehman Jr, Reactions to women in ministry: a survey of English Baptist Church members, *The Baptist Quarterly*, 31, pp 302-320, 1986. See also Sexism, organisational maintenance and localism: a research note, *Sociological Analysis*, 48, pp 274-282, 1987.
34 N. Nason-Clark, Clerical attitudes towards appropriate roles for women in church and society: an empirical investigation of Anglican, Methodist and Baptist clergy in Southern England, unpublished PhD dissertation, London School of Economics, 1984.
35 E.C. Lehman Jr, *Women Clergy in England: sexism, modern consciousness and church viability*, New York, The Edwin Mellen Press, 1987.
36 N. Nason-Clark, Ordaining women as priests: religious vs sexist explanations for clerical attitudes, *Sociological Analysis*, 48, pp 259-273, 1987.
37 A. Aldridge, Men, women and clergymen: opinion and authority in sacred organisations, *Sociological Review*, 37, pp 43-64, 1989.
38 L.J. Francis, The personality characteristics of Anglican ordinands: feminine men and masculine women, *Personality and Individual Differences*, 12, pp 1133-1140, 1991.
39 H.J. Eysenck and S.B.G. Eysenck, *Manual of the Eysenck Personality Questionnaire*, London, Hodder and Stoughton, 1975.
40 L.J. Francis, Male and female clergy in England, *Journal of Empirical Theology*, 5, pp 31-38, 1992.
41 S.B.G. Eysenck, H.J. Eysenck and P. Barrett, A revised version of the psychoticism scale, *Personality and Individual Differences*, 6, pp 21-29, 1985.
42 L. Stevens, Different voice/different voices: Anglican women in ministry, *Review of Religious Research*, 30, pp 262-275, 1989.
43 C. Gilligan, *In a Different Voice*, Cambridge, Massachusetts, Harvard University Press, 1982.
44 See for example L. Kohlberg, The development of children's orientations toward a moral order: 1, sequence in the development of human thought, *Vita Humana*, 6, pp 11-33, 1963 or *The Philosophy of Moral Development*, New York, Harper and Row, 1981.
45 B. Fullalove, The ministry of women in the Church of England (1919-1970) Parts 1 and 2, *The Modern Churchman*, 29, pp 35-44 and 41-50, 1987.
46 K. Burn, *The Calling of Kath Burn*, Chichester, Angel Press, 1988.
47 E. Canham, *Pilgrimage to Priesthood*, London, SPCK, 1983.
48 Women lawfully ordained abroad: report of a working group appointed by the standing committee (GS415), 1979.
49 *Draft Women Ordained Abroad Measure* (GS598), 1983.
50 Legislation which was deemed to come under Article 8 meant that it had to achieve a two thirds majority in the House of Bishops, Clergy and Laity.
51 *Draft Women Ordained Abroad Measure and Draft Amending Canon Number 13* (GS716), 1986. The women ordained abroad measure

never made it beyond draft form. For a full discussion see J Field-Bibb, *Women Towards Priesthood*, Cambridge University Press, 1991.
52 For further details see *Deacons in the Ministry of the Church*, A Report to the House of Bishops of the General Synod of the Church of England, (GS802), 1988, London, Church House Publishing. (The Portsmouth Report.)
53 Advisory Council for the Church's Ministry, *Women in Ministry: a study*, London, Church House Publishing, 1968.
54 *The Ordination of Women to the Diaconate* (GS549), report by the Standing Committee, London, Church House Publishing, 1982.
55 A. Aldridge, In the absence of the minister: structures of subordination in the role of deaconess in the Church of England, *Sociology*, 21, pp 377-392, 1987.
56 Christian Howard produced *The Ordination of Women to the Priesthood: consultative document for the General Synod* (GS104) in 1972. Twelve years later she produced *The Ordination of Women to the Priesthood: further report* (GSMisc 198).
57 The Movement for the Ordination of Women was officially founded in 1979. The first moderator was Stanley Booth-Clibborn (Bishop of Manchester).
58 The Association for the Apostolic Ministry 1986, brought together Evangelicals and Anglo-Catholics.
59 Until 1992 Margaret Hewitt was President of Women against the Ordination of Women. According to *The Telegraph* 6 November 1992 this group was a well kept secret who held a great deal of power within the General Synod.
60 Cost of Conscience had a membership of ordained clergy.
61 *The Ordination of Women to the Priesthood: the scope of the legislation* (GS738), 1986.
62 Margaret Webster, *A New Strength a New Song: the journey to women's priesthood*, London, Mowbray, 1994. This book is written by an active member of the Movement for the Ordination of Women and links the movement's perspective with the whole debate surrounding women's path to priesthood.
63 *The Ordination of Women to the Priesthood: first report by the House of Bishops* (GS764), 1987.
64 S. Gill, *Women and the Church of England: from the eighteenth century to the present*, London, SPCK, 1994. This book provides a thorough overview of the issue from an historical perspective.
65 The verbatim record of the debate was produced by Church House Publishing in 1993: *The Ordination of Women to the Priesthood: the Synod debate 11 November 1992*.
66 *The Ordination of Women to the Priesthood: a second report by the House of Bishops of the General Synod of the Church of England* (GS829), 1988.
67 *Draft Priests (ordination of women) Measure* (GS830), 1988.
68 *Draft Canon C4B (of women priests)* (GS831), 1988.

69 *Draft Amending Canon Number 13* (GS832), 1988.
70 *Draft Ordination of Women (financial provisions) Measure* (GS833), 1988.
71 K. Armstrong, *The End of Silence*, London, Fourth Estate, 1993.
72 P.N. Hague *Questionnaire Design*, London, Kogan Page, 1993.
73 In the service for the Ordination of Deacons in *The Alternative Service Book, 1980*, London, Hodder and Stoughton, p. 345 where the bishop asks the candidates, 'Do you believe, so far as you know your own heart that God has called you to the office and work of a deacon in his church?'
74 J.W. Carroll, B. Hargrove and A.T. Lummis, found that the majority of both men and women entered ministry as the result of a 'call from God'. *Women of the Cloth: a new opportunity for the churches*, New York, Harper and Row, 1983.
75 For a discussion on selection, see Advisory Council for the Church's Ministry, *Selection for Ministry: a report on criteria*, London, Church House, 1983. Advisory Board of Ministry, *The Report of a Working Party on Criteria for Selection for Ministry in the Church of England*, 1993.
76 M. Robbins and L.J. Francis, The selection process: comparing the experiences of stipendiary and non-stipendiary Anglican clergywomen in the UK, unpublished paper.
77 There is a selectors handbook published by the Advisory Board of Ministry.
78 For a recent discussion of the relationship between theological college and training incumbent see K. Randall, Where are you coming from? A review of theological college hand-over days, *British Journal of Theological Education*, 7, pp 18-28, 1995.
79 A classic example of a study conducted among ordinands is provided by R. Towler and A. P. M. Coxon, *The Fate of the Anglican Clergy*, London, Macmillan, 1979. A more recent example is provided by L.J. Francis, The personality characteristics of Anglican ordinands: feminine men and masculine women? *Personality and Individual Differences*, 12, pp 1133-1140, 1991.
80 A number of studies have found that first appointments for clergywomen tend to be fairly straightforward, compared with subsequent appointments which cause more difficulty. See for example, P.D. Nesbitt, Dual ordination tracks: differential benefits and costs for men and women clergy, *Sociology of Religion*, 54, pp 13-30, 1993 or J.W. Carroll, B. Hargrove and A.T. Lummis, *Women of the Cloth: a new opportunity for the churches*, New York, Harper and Row, 1983.
81 *Training of Training Incumbents* (Part 1), Advisory Council for the Church's Ministry, Occasional paper number 10, 1982.
82 According to the official figures in December 1993 the 737 full-time diocesan women deacons were deployed as follows: 583 as assistant curates or parish deacons, 47 as deacons-in-charge, 40 as team

ministers, 9 as cathedral clergy, and 58 in non-parochial appointments. See *Church Statistics: some facts and figures about the Church of England: 1994*, London, Central Board of Finance of the Church of England, 1994, p 112.

83 See, for example, E.C. Lehman Jr's papers on contact theory: Patterns of lay resistance to women in ministry, *Sociological Analysis*, 41, pp 317-338, 1981; Research on lay church members attitudes toward women clergy: an assessment, *Review of Religious Research*, 28, pp 319-329, 1987.

84 For a discussion of clergy marriages in contemporary society see M. Kirk and T. Leary, *Holy Matrimony? an explanation of marriage and ministry*, Oxford, Lynx, 1994.

85 J.W. Carroll, B. Hargrove and A.T. Lummis, *Women of the Cloth: a new opportunity for the churches*, New York, Harper and Row, 1983, found that there are problems associated with making friendships within parishes in that such friendships can be perceived by other members of the laity as exclusive.

86 The case that women prefer a collaborative style of ministry is maintained, for example, by M. Long-Ice, *Clergywomen and their World Views: calling for a new age*, London, Praeger, 1987 and N. Nason-Clark, Clerical attitudes towards appropriate roles for women in church and society: an empirical investigation of Anglican, Methodist and Baptist clergy in Southern England, unpublished PhD dissertation, London School of Economics, 1984.

87 Recent studies of stress and burnout in ministry are provided by J.A. Sanford, *Ministry Burnout*, London, Arthur James, 1982; M.A. Coate, *Clergy Stress: the hidden conflicts in ministry*, London, SPCK, 1989; B. Fletcher, *Clergy under Stress*, London, Mowbray, 1990; J. Davey, *Burnout: stress in the ministry*, Leominster, Gracewing, 1995.

88 The distinction is made, for example, between emotional exhaustion, depersonalisation and personal accomplishment by C. Maslach and S.E. Jackson, *Maslach Burnout Inventory*, Palo Alto, California, Consulting Psychologists Press, 1986.

89 The case that women express ministry differently from men is argued, for example, by M. Long-Ice, *Clergywomen and their World Views: calling for a new age*, London, Praeger, 1987. See also N. Nason-Clark, Clerical attitudes towards appropriate roles for women in church and society: an empirical investigation of Anglican, Methodist and Baptist clergy in Southern England, unpublished PhD dissertation, London School of Economics, 1984.

90 However, Lehman found that evidence for differences in leadership style is only present under very specific conditons. See E.C. Lehman Jr, *Gender and Work: the case of the clergy*, New York, State University of New York Press, 1993. Klein found in her study that differences were not gender specific. See M.C. Klein, The influence of gender on pastoral leadership style, *On the Way*, 11, pp 25-37, 1994.

91 A discussion of various classification systems for clergy roles is presented by L.J. Francis and R. Rodger, The influence of personality on clergy role prioritization, role influence, conflict and dissatisfaction with ministry, *Personality and Individual Differences*, 16, pp 947-957, 1994.

92 The view of the Anglican clergy providing leadership within the wider community is offered by D. Davies, C. Watkins and M. Winter, *Church and Religion in Rural England*, Edinburgh, T. and T. Clark, 1991.

93 Recent insights into the pastoral role of the clergy are provided by S. Pattison, *A Critique of Pastoral Care* (second edition), London, SCM, 1993.

94 The work of clergy among children and teenagers is discussed by recent reports from the General Synod Board of Education: *Children in the Way: new directions for the Church's children*, London, National Society/Church House Publishing, 1988; *All God's Children? children's evangelism in crisis*, London, National Society/Church House Publishing, 1991; *Youth A Part: young people and the church*, London, National Society/Church House Publishing, 1996.

95 A discussion of the liturgical role of the deacon is provided by A. Burnham, The liturgical ministry of a deacon, in C. Hall (ed.), *The Deacon's Ministry*, Leominster, Gracewing, 1991, pp 67-87.

96 A discussion of the pastoral role of the occasional offices is provided by W. Carr, *Brief Encounters: pastoral ministry through the occasional offices*, London, SPCK, 1985.

97 Two discussions of the inclusive language issue are provided by V. Faull and J. Sinclair, *Count us in: inclusive language in liturgy*, Bramcote, Grove Books, 1986; A report by the Liturgical Commission of the General Synod of the Church of England, *Making Women Visible: the use of inclusive language with the ASB*, London, Church House Publishing, 1989.

98 See for example C. Treasure, *Walking on Glass: women deacons speak out*, London, SPCK, 1991, particularly chapter 3. See also M. Furlong, *A Dangerous Delight: women and power in the church*, London, SPCK, 1991.

99 See, for example, S. Dowell and J. Williams, *Bread, Wine and Women: the ordination debate in the Church of England*, London, Virago Press, 1994. For an account of the debate from the perspective of the Movement for the Ordination of Women (MOW) see M. Webster, *A New Strength a New Song: the journey to women's priesthood*, London, Mowbray, 1994.

100 A number of prominent figures left the Church of England for the Roman Catholic Church including Ann Widdecombe and John Gummer. 'Gummer rallies only 21 votes, and may quit church: women priests backed as MPs reject warnings' read the Guardian on 30 October 1993 in reference to the vote in the House of Commons.

101 In an effort to deal with the problems created by the legislation the

bishops put together the Manchester Statement in 1993. This statement set out the idea of the two integrities within the Church of England: one that can accept the ordination of women to the priesthood, and one that cannot in conscience accept the ordination of women. It also proposed 'provincial episcopal visitors' for clergy and laity who could not accept the ordination of women priests.

102 Despite the argument against the ordination of women that it would create problems in closer relationship with the Roman Catholic Church, it is clear from Ruth A Wallace's research, *They Call Her Pastor: a new role for Catholic women*, Albany, New York, State University of New York Press, 1992, that in effect the Roman Catholic Church has women filling the short fall of male priests and in effect carrying out the role of pastor.

103 Bishop Penny Jamieson had been on a number of trips to the UK and was in many ways held up as a role model of what women in ordained ministry could achieve. Her book *Living at the edge: sacrament and solidarity in leadership*, London, Mowbray, 1997, gives an interesting account of her ministry as bishop. As far as we are aware there has yet to be any empirical work published on women in the episcopate. However, Paula D. Nesbitt has undertaken a quantitative study of those who attended the 1998 Lambeth conference.

104 See, for example, J.L. Herman, Item writing techniques, in J.P. Keeves (ed.), *Educational Research, Methodology and Measurement: an international handbook*, Oxford, Pergamon Press, 1988, pp 358-363.

105 A well known example of 'yes' and 'no' responses is presented by the Eysenck Personality Questionnaire. See H.J. Eysenck and S.B.G. Eysenck, *Manual of the Eysenck Personality Questionnaire*, London, Hodder and Stoughton, 1975.

106 The third category was added, for example, by the more recent Eysenck Personality Profile. See H.J. Eysenck, P. Barrett, G. Wilson and C. Jackson, Primary trait measurement of the twenty one components of the PEN system, *European Journal of Psychological Assessment*, 8, pp 109-117, 1992.

107 See R. Likert, A technique for the measurement of attitudes, *Archives of Psychology*, pp 140, 1-55, 1932.

108 The Revised Eysenck Personality Questionnaire is described by S.B.G. Eysenck, H.J. Eysenck and P. Barrett, A revised version of the psychoticism scale, *Personality and Individual Differences*, 6, pp 21-29, 1985.

109 See C.J.F. Rutledge, Parochial clergy today: a study of role, personality and burnout among clergy in the Church of England, unpublished MPhil dissertation, University of Wales, Lampeter.

110 See, for example, L.J. Francis and M. Robbins, Differences in the personality profile of stipendiary and non-stipendiary female Anglican parochial clergy in Britain and Ireland, *Contact*, 119, pp 26-32, 1996; M. Robbins, L.J. Francis and C.J.F. Rutledge, The personality

characteristics of Anglican stipendiary parochial clergy: gender differences revisited, *Personality and Individual Differences*, 23, pp 199-204, 1997.
111 A further detailed examination of the response rate to the survey is published by L.J. Francis and M. Robbins, Survey response rate as a function of age: are female clergy different? *Psychological Reports*, 77, pp 499-506, 1995.
112 See L.J. Francis and M. Robbins, A woman's voice in a man's world: listening to women clergy in the Church in Wales before the vote, *Contemporary Wales*, 9, pp 74-90, 1996.
113 For discussion of gender differences in religion see C.D. Field, Adam and Eve: gender in the English Free Church constituency, *Journal of Ecclesiastical History*, 44, pp 63-79, 1993; L.J. Francis, The psychology of gender differences in religion: a review of empirical research, *Religion*, 27, pp 81-96, 1997.
114 The semantic differential grid has its origin in C.E. Osgood, G.J. Saci and P.H. Tannenbaum, *The Measurement of Meaning*, Urbana, Illinois, University of Illinios Press, 1957.
115 For the importance of factors like age in predicting individual differences in clergy attitudes see L.J. Francis and S.H. Jones (eds), *Psychological Perspectives on Christian Ministry*, Leominster, Gracewing, 1996.
116 A. Aldridge, Slaves to no sect: the Anglican clergy and liturgical change, *Sociological Review*, 34, pp 357-380, 1986.
117 See, for example, the classic study by S. Ranson, A. Brynman and B. Hinings, *Clergy, Ministers and Priests*, London, Routlege and Kegan Paul, 1977.
118 For discussion of the Catholic wing see F. Penhale, *Catholics in Crisis*, London, Mowbray, 1986; W.S.F. Pickering, *Anglo-Catholicism: a study in religious ambiguity*, London, SPCK, 1989.
119 For discussion of the Evangelical wing see M. Saward, *Evangelicals on the Move*, London, Mowbray, 1987; D.J. Tidball, *Who are the Evangelicals?* London, Marshall Pickering, 1994.
120 For discussion of the middle way see P. Walker, *Rediscovering the Middle Way*, London, Mowbray, 1988.
121 L.J. Francis and D.W. Lankshear, *In the Catholic Way*, London, National Society, 1995.
122 L.J. Francis and D.W. Lankshear, *In the Evangelical Way*, London, National Society, 1995.
123 L.J. Francis and T.H. Thomas, Are Anglo Catholic priests more feminine? a study among male Anglican clergy, *Pastoral Sciences*, 15, pp 15-22, 1996.
124 For a discussion of non-stipendiary ministry see J.M.M. Francis and L.J. Francis (eds), *Tentmaking: perspectives on self-supporting ministry*, Leominster, Gracewing, 1998.

INDEX

Advisory Board of Ministry 23, 243
Advisory Council for the Church's Ministry 23, 239-240, 242, 243
Aldridge, A. 11, 17, 48, 241-242, 247
Amir, Y. 240
Armstrong, K. 243
Article 8 15-16, 241
Association for the Apostolic Ministry 19, 242

Baptism(s) 33-34, 96, 166-168, 170, 171, 181-184, 186, 243
Barrett, P. 241, 246
Bem, S.L. 8, 9, 14, 240
Bible 10, 35, 188-194
Bock, N.E. 7, 240
Booth-Clibborn, S. 242
Bowlby, R. 18
Brynman, A. 247
Burn, K. 16, 241
Burnham, A. 245

California Test of Mental Maturity 3, 239
Canham, E. 15, 241
Cardwell, S.W. 3, 239
Carroll, J.W. 3, 239-240, 243-244
Carpenter, D.C. 4-5, 239
Carr, W. 245
Children 34, 127-128, 131, 174-180, 236, 241, 245
Clark, W.W. 239
Coger, M. 4, 239
Collaborative ministry 22, 30, 138-137, 140-142, 233
Community 33-34, 78, 131, 150-151, 158, 160-165, 174, 245
Confirmation 33, 49, 166-167, 171
Congregation 3-4, 6-8, 10-11, 13, 23, 28, 35, 58, 115-121, 129, 188-189 191-195, 210, 212, 232, 236

Contact Hypothesis 6, 11, 240
Cost of Conscience 19, 242
Counselling 33, 166-173, 236
Coxon, A.P.M. 243

Davies, D. 245
Dittes, J.E. 239
Dowell, S. 245
Dual ordination tract 5, 239, 243

Ecumenism 37, 212-214
Education(al) 5, 7, 9, 13, 44-45, 144, 233-234, 243, 245-246
Ekhardt, B.N. 8, 240
Ervin, C. 240
Eysenck, H.J. 12, 14, 40, 241, 246
Eysenck, S.B.G. 241, 246

Family 6, 22, 29, 56, 81, 122-128, 136, 159, 232
Faull, V. 245
Field, C.D. 247
Field-Bibb, J. 242
Flagg, K. 8, 240
Francis, L.J. 12, 49, 241, 243, 245-247
Francis, J.M.M. 247
Fullalove, B. 241
Funeral(s) 34, 96, 172, 181-187, 236
Furlong, M. 245

General Synod 14-21, 36-37, 204, 211-213, 215, 217, 220, 222, 239, 242, 245
Gill, S. 20, 242
Gilligan, C. 12, 241
God 23, 35, 44, 51-53, 56, 58-61, 93, 137, 151, 158, 188-195, 204-211, 237, 243, 245
Goldsmith, W.M. 8, 240
Gough, H.G. 239
Gummer, J. 245

Hague, P.N. 243
Hall, C. 239, 245
Hargrove, B. 3, 239-240, 243-244
Heilbrun, A.B. Jr, 239
Helmreich, R. 240
Herman, J.L. 246
Hewitt, M. 242
Hinings, B. 247
Howard, C. 242
Hunt, R.A. 239
Husband(s) 29, 77, 92, 97, 122, 127-128, 159, 203
Hymn(s) 35, 188-195

Inclusive language 22, 35, 188-195, 236, 245

Jackson, C. 246
Jackson, D.N. 244
Jackson, S.E. 240
Jamieson, P. 227, 246
Jones, S.H. 247

Keeves, J.P. 246
Kirk, M. 244
Klein, M.C. 244
Kohlberg, L. 12, 241

Lankshear, D.W. 49, 247
Leary, T. 244
Lehman, E.C. Jr, 6, 8, 10-11, 240-241, 244
Likert, R. 39, 47, 246
Liturgy 35, 187-189, 245
Liturgical 22, 34, 48, 181-187, 234-235, 245, 247
Long Ice, M. 5, 239, 244
Lummis, A.T. 3, 239-240, 243-244

Maslach, C. 244
McClean, D. 18-20
Ministry Style(s) 4, 8, 14, 30, 137-138, 141, 233
Minnesota Multiphasic Personality Inventory 3
Money 32, 77, 152-157
Movement for the Ordination of

Women 18-19, 242, 245

Nason-Clark, N. 10-11, 241, 244
Nesbitt, P.D. 5, 239, 243, 246

Osgood, C.E. 247

Parishioners 4, 22, 28, 31, 115-118, 120, 133, 136, 142, 151, 165, 172-173, 179, 232
Partner 26-27, 29, 42, 48, 79-81, 83, 92, 99-101, 122-128, 159, 232
Pattison, S. 245
Penfold, S. 9, 240
Penhale, F. 247
Personality Research Form 8, 240
Pickering, W.S.F. 247

Randall, K. 243
Ranson, S. 247
Robbins, M. 243, 246-247
Rodger, R. 245
Roof, W.C. 10, 240
Royle, M.H. 7, 240
Rutledge, C.J.F. 246-247

Saci, G.J. 247
Sacrament(s) 19, 86, 246
Sacramental 143, 187
Sacramentally 10
Saward, M. 247
Selection 3, 22-25, 60, 62-69, 87, 123, 229, 230, 243
Selectors 24, 62-69, 243
Service(s)(book) 34-36, 59, 113, 172, 181, 187-195, 204, 236, 239-240, 243
Sinclair, J. 245
Spiritual director(s) 167-168, 170-171, 173
Stevens, L. 12-13, 241
Stapp, J. 240
Stress(es) 4, 7, 13, 22, 31, 144-153 233-234, 239-240, 244
Sullivan, E.T. 239

Tannenbaum, P.H. 247

Teacher(s) 33, 45, 160-165
Teenagers 34, 49, 166, 174-177, 179, 245
Texas Social Behaviour Inventory 8, 240
Theological School Inventory 3, 239
Thomas, T.H. 49, 247
Tidball, D.J. 247
Tiegs, E.W. 239
Towler, R. 243
Treasure, C. 9, 240, 245

Visitor(s) 160-164, 235, 246
Vocation 23-24, 36-37, 51, 59-60, 62, 68, 153, 196-197, 199, 201-202, 210, 212-213, 215-217, 219-220, 229, 237-238

Walker, P. 247
Wallace, R.A. 246

Watkins, C. 245
Webster, M. 19, 242, 245
Weddings 34, 96, 181-183, 185, 187
Widdecombe, A. 245
Wife (wives) 11, 26-27, 29, 79, 80, 83, 99-100, 102, 104, 106, 122, 127, 203, 230
Williams, J. 245
Wilson, G. 246
Winter, M. 245
Women Against the Ordination of Women 19, 242
Women's groups 174-178, 180
Worship(ping) 17, 34, 78, 181-182, 184, 186, 188

Young people 78, 174, 245
Youth groups 34, 174